D0848625

Constitutional

Failure

CONSTITUTIONAL THINKING

Jeffrey K. Tulis and Sanford Levinson, *Editors*

Constitutional
Failure

Sotirios A. Barber

University Press of Kansas

Published by the University Press of Kansas (Lawrence, Kansas 66045), which
was organized by the Kansas Board of Regents and is operated and funded by
Emporia State University, Fort Hays State University, Kansas State University,
Pittsburg State University, the University of Kansas, and Wichita State University

Library of Congress Cataloging-in-Publication Data

Barber, Sotirios A., author.

Constitutional failure / Sotirios Barber.

pages cm

Includes index.

ISBN 978-0-7006-2007-4 (hardback)

ISBN 978-0-7006-2044-9 (ebook)

1. Constitutional law—United States. I. Title.

KF4550.B259 2014

42.73—dc23

2014026578

British Library Cataloguing-in-Publication Data is available.

Printed in the United States of America

10 9 8 7 6 5 4 3 2 1

The paper used in this publication is recycled and contains 30 percent
postconsumer waste. It is acid free and meets the minimum requirements of
the American National Standard for Permanence of Paper for Printed Library
Materials z39.48-1992.

For Leah and Alex

Contents

Foreword

In recent years, numerous books have appeared that detail the breakdown of American government. With provocative titles and themes such as *The Rise and Decline of the American Republic* or *It's Even Worse Than It Looks*, political scientists, legal academics, journalists, and even politicians are increasingly concerned that our political system is failing under twenty-first-century conditions. Yet for all the attention to our serious political problems, few thinkers have taken up the question of constitutional failure itself. What does it mean for the Constitution to fail? This is a question for which an answer is *assumed* by many, but articulated and defended by few. The title of the book that you hold in your hands may not be provocative, but compared to other books on the contemporary crisis of government, this one offers the most original and provocative *argument*. This is a book that unsettles conventional wisdom and fashionable academic opinion.

Institutional breakdown is not the mark of constitutional failure, Barber argues. Instead, the impossibility of reform defines constitutional failure. Reform becomes impossible when citizens lose or lack the healthy political attitudes and civic understanding necessary to recognize and contend with serious political problems. The implications of this conception of constitutional failure are stunning: the Articles of Confederation was not a constitutional failure, says Barber, because its citizens were competent to make a new constitution. The promise of the Constitution evidences the success of the Articles of Confederation. The Civil War was not a failure because it was the occasion for a refounding of the American regime. For Barber, the failure of the Constitution to remedy its defects peacefully revealed a deeper success in the fact that the nineteenth-century constitutional culture produced a statesman of uncommon ability and a citizenry that could understand, appreciate, and support such extraordinary leadership. Moreover, late-twentieth-century America—a time of unprecedented prosperity—reveals a profound constitutional failure to the extent that the American people have lost the attitudes, knowledge, and virtue characteristic of America's citizenry at its origins and in its darkest domestic hour. To sum up Barber's thesis in a nutshell: when you thought American constitutions had failed, they succeeded; and when you thought the Constitution was succeeding, it was actually failing.

Barber begins this book by noting the paradox that Americans love their Constitution even as they dislike their government. They venerate the Constitution while lacking respect for Congress, the president, and increasingly the Supreme Court. Barber urges a new kind of veneration—veneration of founding thinking rather than worship of a document, persona, or flag. Returning to the founding way of thinking, but leaving open the conclusion one might reach, raises for us the possibility that the Constitution is its own source of failure. Barber asks us to reconsider the merits of our reliance on institutional design to replace the role of virtue and character in leaders and citizens.

At first one gets the impression that Barber thinks the Antifederalists possessed the better understanding of constitutional failure because they had such doubts about the Federalists' new idea of separation of powers. But Barber also traces weaknesses in our contemporary thinking to the false idea that ours is and should be primarily a negative-liberties constitution—a design built on the idea that limits to governmental power are the central or most fundamental feature of our Constitution. This conception was originally an Antifederal idea. The idea that ours is fundamentally a Constitution skeptical of governmental power, and of national power especially, has rendered much contemporary constitutional theory incoherent. Barber shows that the fundamental feature of any constitution must be a positive purpose to solve some problem or accomplish some plan. If the *fundamental* purpose of government were to limit itself, one would have no reason to want a government in the first place. One would be better off without government. The Federalists understood this point and stressed that the Constitution creates power to accomplish legitimate public purposes. Of course, one needs to worry about the possible abuse of power, but a sound constitution provides all the power necessary to accomplish its aims. The Federalists thought the problem of too much power could be solved by creating contending institutions and contending powers rather than limiting the power of government as a whole.

Thus, Barber shows how the Antifederalists and the Federalists were both wrong—and both right. He upends the common understanding of their thought by showing that the Antifederal critique of a constitution devoid of civic education was correct, but not for the reasons they offered. Civic education and virtue were necessary not primarily to protect the citizenry and the states from the tyranny of the national government, but more to make the national government work. He shows that the Federalists were right to stress the need to create power to accomplish common political purposes, but they were wrong to ignore the need for a much more robust civic understanding and engagement to enable government and to hold it accountable.

Barber does not place as much explicit emphasis on the Antifederalists and Federalists, per se, as I have just done. Rather he shows how basic orientations captured by their original contest—the *kind of thinking* they displayed—can better connect contemporary constitutional theory to the crisis of governance today than can observations limited by categories and arguments more prominent in the writings of constitutional theorists today. Readers will thus be treated to a superb overview and introduction to the field of constitutional theory even as the book focuses on the specific topic of failure. This book offers an accessible overview of Barber's large and rich body of work on the meaning of the American Constitution.

Barber's broad-ranging account of constitutional failure and contemporary constitutional theory shows citizens the skill and knowledge they need to repair what ails America. Barber is only cautiously optimistic that America can be repaired. The book ends with a sharp critique of academic constitutional thinking. Barber shows that ordinary citizens, for all their ignorance and inexperience, still possess more common sense than many, perhaps most, academic constitutional thinkers. Ordinary citizens act on the belief that justice and the common good are real aspects of the world about which we disagree and for which we seek better answers.

Many academics, including my esteemed coeditor of this series, Sanford Levinson, are skeptical that there are moral truths to seek. Barber offers a pointed rebuttal to academic moral skepticism and shows how that skeptical attitude further inclines the Constitution to failure. While Barber seeks to make citizens more sophisticated, he seeks to bring sophisticated academics back to common sense.

We hope that the inclusion of Sotirios Barber's book in this series and our recognition that it is a powerful argument, despite our disagreements with it, displays the kind of healthy civic attitude he would welcome.

Jeffrey K. Tulis
Coeditor, *Constitutional Thinking*

Preface

Americans have a low opinion of their government but a high opinion of the U.S. Constitution. These opinions make a coherent pair only if the Constitution is merely a law, in this case a law that the government may be failing to observe. One could hardly blame the law for the failure of its subjects to follow the law. Yet this reasoning doesn't quite apply to the Constitution because the Constitution is more than a law. It is also a design or plan of government, and one would think that if a government is failing it has a defective design. In this case praising the Constitution and condemning the government would make little sense.

You could say in response that the nation's favorable view of the Constitution is a good thing even if a favorable view of the Constitution makes little sense paired with an unfavorable view of the government. Political opinions can be salutary even if they don't make sense in all respects. The Constitution is at least a symbol of political unity, and as a symbol of unity its value rises with the disunity that's largely responsible for the government's failure. Venerating the Constitution is thus a good idea not despite political dysfunction but because of it.

This would be an apt response up to a point, but only up to a point. A symbol of unity has value only if it either reflects or contributes to actual unity, not if it fails to arrest or even exacerbates disunity. If the Constitution should exacerbate or fail to arrest disunity, veneration of the Constitution would be a bad idea. Veneration of the Constitution would then be blindness to its defects, and the blindness would preclude the effort to correct the defects. Facing and correcting constitutional defects is something Americans once did quite well. They did it in 1789 and again in the 1860s, and they earned the world's admiration in the process.

On the other hand, there'd be no point in facing the Constitution's defects without some realistic hope of reform—that is, unless some part or stratum of the community was sufficiently capable and dedicated to the task of leading the nation to constitutional change. If "capable of leading the nation" means, in part, "trusted by the nation to lead," America is in trouble. Polls show the absence of any such leadership stratum among any of the nation's institutions, governmental and nongovernmental. The only institution in which a majority of Americans express confidence today is the military, and the country (or part of it) accepted the military as an instrument of constitutional change only during Reconstruction. We can seriously doubt, therefore, that deliberate constitutional change of any magnitude is possible prior to trauma that might befall a people but that no people would ever wish for itself. So as a practical matter—a matter on which any part of the nation with a prayer of moving the whole is prepared to act—we're almost certainly stuck with what we've got.

To appreciate just how profoundly we're stuck with what we've got, reflect on all that constitutional failure must mean. The American Constitution is a document, ink on parchment, under special archival glass. Though we talk about "living constitution," that's just a metaphor; no one believes this document is a thing that can act. And since it can't act, the Constitution itself can't succeed or fail, for failure and success are properties of actions and cognate phenomena, like activities and practices. When we say the Constitution succeeds or fails, therefore, we're talking about the government whose outline the Constitution describes. And since the government is supposed to represent all of us, we mean ultimately that the nation succeeds or fails, that we as a political community succeed or fail. Constitutional failure is thus the failure of a culture. And constitutional reform must therefore be nothing short of cultural reform.

Viewed against this fact virtually every current proposal for constitutional reform appears stunningly inadequate. For all but one or two of these proposals focus on governmental institutions and assume that reform is basically a matter of making institutions more responsive to democratic opinion. Few of today's observers seem to see constitutional reform as a matter of cultural reform. Yet there could be method in this error. Perhaps we should keep the conversation going even if, for the moment, we're talking about the wrong thing. We have no hope of eventually talking about the right thing if we stop the conversation altogether, and facing a problem as daunting as the real problem may stop the conversation altogether. Constitutional reform is all but impossible for us precisely because constitutional reform for us would mean cultural reform, and we wouldn't need cultural reform if we were capable of accomplishing it through a process of public discussion.

Why, then, write about the real problem of constitutional failure? Why trouble to read about it? One answer lies in what we seem to be: creatures who value truth regardless of the practical payoff. Another answer is that we can't rule out a practical payoff. Lightning strikes. It struck in America in the late 1780s, in the early 1860s, and in the early 1930s. Should it strike again, we might want to know what constitutional failure and success mean and how to think about them.

Acknowledgments

The National Endowment for the Humanities and Notre Dame's College of Arts and Letters extended sabbatical support that made this essay possible. Friends with whom I debated key portions of my argument over the years include Jim Fleming, Steve Macedo, Walter Murphy, and Ross Jacobs. Karen Flax and Jeff Tulis read the penultimate draft and saved me from numerous errors of style and content. Larisa Martin smoothed the path to publication, and Fred Woodward prodded me along it. Warmest thanks to all.

I

Why Talk about Constitutional Failure?

This book addresses a paradox: Americans have lost faith in their government, yet they revere the constitution that established their government and continues to structure its operations. I argue in this book that this paradox is due to a misunderstanding of what the Constitution is. I believe, moreover, that this misunderstanding is a fatal misunderstanding. I argue that recovering the lost understanding (the "lost constitutionalism of the framers," if you prefer) requires supplementing, perhaps even rejecting, the framers' own strategy for constitutional maintenance. The framers' strategy is called "checks and balances," and no idea is more associated with American constitutionalism than "checks and balances." If recovering the framers' constitutionalism actually did require rejecting this idea, then recovering the framers' constitutionalism would require rejecting the framers' constitution. One paradox would thus replace another. To resolve this last paradox, I'd have to show that the American Constitution is less a document—and the behavioral theory behind it—than a political culture, and that constitutional failure is less an institutional than an attitudinal matter. More specifically, I'd have to show that constitutional survival in America depends on attitudes like patriotism, trust, and magnanimity, and that relying mainly on checking and balancing self-serving attitudes guarantees eventual constitutional failure.

The Initial Paradox

Over the last half century Americans have grown increasingly doubtful about their government's ability to meet the country's economic, social, and environmental challenges. Congress has been the chief focus of this worry, due mainly to undemocratic aspects of the Senate's composition and operation, a practice of financing electoral campaigns that beggars Congress to special interests, and ideological division that makes it impossible for Congress to function as a deliberative body. In June 2013, Gallup reported that only 10 percent of the public had "a great deal or quite a lot" of confidence in Congress, with 52 percent expressing "very little" to no confidence, and 37 percent having only "some" confidence in Congress. This contrasts with the 47 percent who voiced "a great deal" or "quite a lot" of confidence in Congress in May 1973. Congress is far from the only worry. Confidence in the presidency as an institution declined from 72 percent in March 1991 to 36 percent in June 2013. And confidence in the Supreme Court declined from an average of 45 percent in the ten-year period from 1973 to 1983 to 34 percent in June 2013.[1] A puzzling element of this situation is the public's esteem for the Constitution. According to the AP–National Constitutional Center Poll of August 2012, 69 percent of the public (down from 74 percent in both 2010 and 2011) considers the Constitution an "enduring document" that does not need to be "modernized."[2]

These figures provoke the question of how Americans can have a good opinion of their Constitution and a bad opinion of their government. Shouldn't opinions of government and constitution rise and fall together? Isn't one supposed to be the plan of the other? *Federalist* 1 calls the Constitution a "plan" of government, a plan for a "good government," one that will facilitate the people's "dignity," "liberty," and "happiness." Because *The Federalist* offers the plan to the public as a remedy for "the insufficiency of the existing federal government" (i.e., the Articles of Confederation), the plan resembles a physician's prescription: follow this plan and you'll do better, says *The Federalist*. Can a prescription be a good one if it's wrong for the patient? And is it wrong to assess the value of a prescription by whether the patient actually improves? The patient did improve in the 1780s and periodically thereafter. But at this writing future prospects for the country don't look good, and the prescription was supposed to be good indefinitely.

True, you can't blame a plan if the patient doesn't follow it. But though the nation has ignored the plan in the past, especially during the Civil War, the patient follows the plan today. Right-wing critics of the New Deal and its successors deny this last proposition. They bemoan the manner in which so-called leftist judges and politicians "rewrote the Constitution," and they dream of "restoring the lost Constitution" of the Coolidge era.[3] But by "the plan" I mean the Constitution's structural provisions—the Constitution's policy-making and adjudicatory procedures, including the procedures for appointing law makers and judges and the rules that specify their tenure of office. Sanford Levinson calls these provisions the Constitution's "hard wired provisions" to distinguish them from the variable standards found mostly in the Bill of Rights and the Civil War Amendments. Structural provisions are "hard wired" because there's little debate about what they prescribe. They don't invite competing conceptions the way "due process" and "freedom of speech" do, and this gives them some insulation from change by judicial interpretation.[4] Right-wing critics of today's national government claim that it has exceeded its authorized powers, usually at the expense of the states; they don't normally claim that national institutions were unlawfully established, or that national politicians occupy their offices illegally, or that officials and institutions employ unlawful procedures. So when they charge that the national government is exceeding its powers they say, in effect, that a constitutional government is doing unauthorized things. By their account, the government remains constitutional even if much of its conduct is unconstitutional.

There are times when officials are said to occupy their offices illegally and proceed to their decisions in unlawful ways. Military tribunals in wartime are frequent targets of these accusations. Congress was an unlawful body when it effectively denied representation to somewhere between a quarter and a third of the nation between 1865 and 1870. The current Senate practice of letting forty-one votes block consideration of politically significant actions and the Hastert Rule among House Republicans effectively defeat the constitutional plan of decision by legislative majorities for routine domestic matters. And for over two centuries many observers have seen the Constitution's ratification itself as an unlawful act. But critics don't normally refer to structural issues like these when they claim the national government exceeds its powers. And if the national government has in fact exceeded its powers, the Constitution deserves some of the blame. More than a set of rules for governing and recruiting governmental officials, the Constitution's hard-wired provisions include rules that define and arrange constitutional offices. These rules can't be understood apart from the assumptions that justify them. Among the Constitution's key structural ideas is the principle of checks and balances. If the national government has exceeded its authority, or to the extent that it has, then the system of checks and balances hasn't done what *The Federalist* says it was designed to do: prevent abuses of authority.

The framers' claim for checks and balances was far from modest. With a measure of pessimism about the patriotism and law-abidingness of Americans generally, *The Federalist* promises that the system of checks and balances will prevent abuses of authority even among officials who are personally inclined to exceed constitutional restraints, because they answer to constituents governed more by their private interests and partisan commitments than their devotion to the Constitution and the common good.[5] So if politicians have exceeded their authority, then the Constitution has failed to that extent, for constitutional checks and balances were supposed to confine institutional actors to their proper spheres. In general, therefore, it's hard to deny that sustained political dysfunction has at least some constitutional connection—even when the political dysfunction results from constitutional infidelity. As Jack Balkin puts it, American politics is conducted within a constitutional framework, and this makes it fair to call the actual conduct of the national government and American political institutions generally as "the Constitution in practice." To say that our politics is failing is to say that the constitution in practice is failing, and therefore so is the Constitution.[6]

Why deny that the Constitution is failing? Why the reluctance to acknowledge the constitutional dimension of our sick politics? The explanation, of course, is that the general public venerates the Constitution and its framers. In *Federalist* 49 James Madison argued that the public's veneration of the Constitution was necessary to political stability because postrevolutionary America couldn't be trusted with the tasks of constitutional repair. All of the nation's existing constitutions, he said, were formed "in the midst" of revolutionary pressures and opportunities that "stifled the ordinary diversity of opinions on great national questions," produced "a universal ardor for new and opposite forms" of government, and promoted "an enthusiastic confidence of the people in their patriotic leaders." "The future," he said, promises no "equivalent security" against "the spirit of party." And therefore, he concluded, it's best to make the Constitution hard to amend and trust time to make it an object of veneration (49:340–341).

Madison's argument is not what it appears to be. It is not really an argument for venerating the Constitution—it is not an argument that the Constitution *deserves* veneration. It is at best an argument for cultivating veneration on the part of those who, if they don't venerate the Constitution, are likely to make it worse. It's also an argument that assumes a measure of constitutional adequacy. It assumes, in other words, that government under the Constitution is approximating constitutional ends more or less as well as can be expected under the circumstances. It assumes further that *some* element in the community is exempt from its scope, for if *all* venerated the Constitution, none could make the calculations and comparisons needed to determine whether the government was actually doing reasonably well. Madison's argument for veneration is thus an argument for pretending to venerate, not really to venerate. As such, it could be a good argument if incorrigible political division or incompetence threatened to make things worse. Pretending to venerate a constitution would also make sense if there were no way to arrest constitutional decline. Why not comfort the dying with illusion if that's the best one can do? So I'm not saying that Madison's argument is a bad argument in all circumstances. In fact, I concede, as I believe all candid observers must, that it's probably (though not quite certainly) a good argument today. Nevertheless, it's a bad argument for those who have any hope for the Constitution's survival. And since the present discussion would be pointless without such hope, it's a bad argument here.

Why Venerating the Constitution Is a Bad Idea

Veneration is a state of mind that takes its value from the value of its object and the consequences of venerating the object. No one would, or should, venerate a golden calf, or the gold in the calf. Yet even regarding things that deserve veneration, veneration has a regrettable side. This is certainly true when the objects of veneration are human things. Veneration implies a kind of blindness: we're blind to the flaws of the persons and things we venerate, insofar as we venerate them. Veneration of the Constitution can blind us to the need for constitutional reform, and a constitution beyond timely reform is a failure waiting to happen. As an abstract matter, instruments are subordinate in value to their ends; the effectiveness of an instrument depends on contingencies beyond the instrument's control; an instrument that can't adapt to changing circumstances will fail when circumstances change; and, sooner or later, circumstances *will* change. This argument of general practical reason is beyond debate. Yet how this argument applies to the Constitution is not at all beyond debate. No one will deny that things change—that is, that matters subject to government change. Most will agree or should agree that the Constitution can't work under any and all conditions, like severe natural disasters and sustained terrorist assault. True, it's been said that the Constitution "is a law for rulers and people, equally in war and in peace, and covers with the shield of its protection all classes of men, at all times, and under all circumstances."[7] But even if anyone seriously believed this, the contrary is implied by the amending provisions of Article V. The very existence of an amending rule in the constitutional document implies that the nation may need to change the Constitution to meet changing conditions, and therefore that at any given point in time the Constitution may not be adequate to conditions. We'd surely agree that no government could control *all* of its natural and political environments and that, therefore, constitutional government can't guarantee the conditions for its successful operation. And since a constitution that hasn't reformed before it's too late is a dead constitution, we can agree that, by definition, *timely* reform (reform that's not too late) and the capacity for timely reform are essential to constitutional survival.

With all this, however, we might still disagree about the Constitution's instrumental nature. That is, we might disagree about the wisdom of understanding the Constitution for what the document's preamble clearly says the Constitution is: a set of means to independently valued goods like justice, the common defense, and the general welfare. As a matter of general practical reason there can be no question that ends are more important than means. But since politics rarely bends to practical reason, one can deny that ends are always more important than means. Ends may not be more important if the meaning of the means is less contested than the meaning of the ends and if the means serve an array of ends broad enough to avoid violence. If we disagree about the meaning of ends like justice and the general welfare, if this disagreement falls short of violence, and if the meaning of justice and the general welfare is pursued through institutional rules that are clear enough to minimize debate about who performs what functions (constitutional means), then in this context means acquire a heightened importance.

Heightened importance or no, however, institutional means remain subordinate to ends. Institutions exist in a context that assumes that they have a point—that they serve some ends or goods—and at no point could we conceive institutional means as ends in themselves. That is, *constitutionalists* can't conceive institutional means as ends in themselves. For propositions within a constitutionalist framework must be consistent with the idea of people establishing a constitution, and no one would establish a government with powers to extinguish life, liberty, and property for the sole pleasure of watching the government operate. The ends, moreover, must be conceived as public goods. Even if individuals agreed to a government solely to secure their personal safety and property, they would have to justify the government to each other in terms broader than their personal interests. They'd have to say the government served some public purpose or common good, like the security of everyone's person and property, a common good that would restrain the private pursuits of each contracting party. (A tyrant might, but no democrat would say to other persons generally: "This is a good government because it secures my property alone.")

Yet the greater importance of constitutional ends remains debatable for a further reason: the Constitution's self-proclaimed status as "supreme Law." Where a set of means is supreme law, means are more than *mere* means. We would need no more than Jefferson's "light and transient causes" to abandon a set of mere means. We would need much more than "light and transient causes" to disregard supreme law. Where means became supreme law, we'd have "to suffer, while Evils are sufferable," acting only when evils approach the unbearable. But as mandatory means became increasingly unbearable they would revert to mere means, and we could and should act by "Right" and "Duty" to replace them with new means—that is, *real* means, means that work.

Such is the understanding of the American creed that Jefferson recorded in the Declaration of Independence. Madison reiterated this understanding in *Federalist* 45 where he recalled the Revolution and said that "the real welfare of the great body of the people, is the supreme object," and that "no form of government whatever," including the Union, "has any other value than as it may be fitted for the attainment of this object" (45:309). Supreme law thus remains instrumental if not *merely* instrumental, and the apparent leap in logic that reduces supreme law to mere means is bridged when we recall that, by its own preamble, the document declares that supreme law was proposed and ratified *as means*. The Federalist supporters of the Constitution justified it as means, and the Antifederalists criticized it as means. So when the "Constitution in practice" ceases to function as means, it is no longer what was ratified, and our right to abandon it, as the framers abandoned the Articles of Confederation, is continuous with the right that established it.

Descending from constitutional logic to constitutional history, we notice an important fact: though Madison urged veneration of the Constitution to his public readership, he said something different in private. In letters to Jefferson of September and October of 1787, five months before he wrote *Federalist* 49, Madison doubted that the Constitution would either achieve "its national objects" or prevent injustices by the states—injustices, he said, "which everywhere excite disgust against the state governments." The chief cause of Madison's pessimism was the refusal of the Constitutional Convention to adopt a general congressional veto over state laws.[8] Madison also saw equal representation of small and large states in the Senate as "a lesser evil" forced on the Convention by political realities. These concessions of the Convention in behalf of state sovereignty ran counter to the large-republic argument that Madison offered in *Federalist* 10 as the heart of his constitutional theory. Such were Madison's worries in the late 1780s. In writing *Federalist* 49, therefore, he was advising reverence for a constitution that he believed to be seriously defective.

Madison's advice poses problems. The first would be identifying its addressees. Who exactly was Madison talking to? Who should cultivate veneration for an admittedly defective constitution? Would the nation be divided into an enlightened few—the Washingtons, the Jeffersons, the Madisons—and a benighted many, with the few finding ways to get around at least some constitutional defects while deceiving the many about the Constitution's virtues for the good of all? Might an elite judicial corps or a standing congressional committee engineer gradual constitutional change through constitutional interpretation? Since Madison was no populist, we can't dismiss some such possibility as consistent with his principles, if not his expectations.

But if we granted such a possibility for argument's sake, other problems would rush in. Constitutional interpretation has its limits. It can change our understanding of ideas like due process and equal protection, but it can't reach the Electoral College, the equal representation of states in the Senate, or a politics that, thanks partly to the framers themselves, emphasizes private interests over public purposes. Once interpretation reaches its limits, an enlightened few would find themselves cultivating reverence for a constitution they knew to be defective. Their question would be what ours is today: How can veneration for a defective constitution correct its defects? How can constitution-worship improve the nation's ability to defend itself from foreign enemies or facilitate the well-being and foster the decency of its people? We're left to wonder, therefore, why anyone would follow Madison's advice in *Federalist* 49. Why would anyone foster reverence for a constitution with potentially fatal defects? Such a constitution wouldn't need reverence; it would need reform. It would need the constructive criticism that precedes reform. It would also need an institution of some sort (necessarily an informal one, as we shall see) that concerned itself with the problem of constitutional reform on a continuing basis, a stable institution to address a standing problem, the possibility of constitutional failure in a world of contingencies.

No one denies that we have to accept and work with a defective constitution, for there's no such thing as a perfect constitution. Elsewhere I've gone to the trouble to show that a perfect constitution is more than practically impossible; it's conceptually impossible, unimaginable.[9] But accepting and working with a constitution is one thing; venerating it is another. Venerating something blinds us to its defects, the opportunities to correct them, and the need to foster the skills, attitudes, and institutions for correcting them. By obscuring the need to cultivate reformist virtues, venerating a constitution defeats hopes for achieving the general welfare at the same time that it risks moral disaster. Let me explain why this is so.

Acknowledging the Constitution's defects, as Madison did to Jefferson, presupposes that the Constitution and the government it establishes are answerable to standards of good policy and right conduct that are not of its making—goods and standards that it can fail to approximate. Acknowledging potential failure thus goes hand in hand with belief in the existence of real goods and real standards—real goods as opposed to merely subjective or conventional goods. The preamble records this understanding perfectly. It refers to things like justice and the general welfare. It places none of these ideas in quotation marks or scare quotes in the manner of today's academic moral skeptics. It contains no hint that, in the manner of today's vaunted patriots, it's talking about some exceptional American conception of justice and other goods. It refers to justice and the general welfare, plain and simple. *Federalist* 1 underscores the idea of justice and welfare, plain and simple, not just American justice and welfare, when it says that failure of the nation's constitutional experiment would "deserve to be considered as the general misfortune of mankind" (1:3).

Venerating a constitution proceeds from a different view of the world. When we think of veneration we think of reverence and therewith of religion and the attitude of believers toward God. We revere God the Creator or the maker, "the Creator of heaven and earth." We can't revere the Constitution that way unless we believe the Constitution is a creator or maker, the maker of America as a nation. Many have said that the Constitution made the nation. But that's not what the Constitution says. That the Constitution made the nation can't be said consistently with the history of the Constitution, as confirmed by the Constitution's preamble and Article VII. This language indicates that a preexisting sociopolitical entity of some sort (an identifiable "We") made the Constitution. God is often revered as the source of American rights. We can't revere the Constitution that way unless we believe it is the source of our rights. Yet the preamble, the Declaration of Independence, and the Ninth Amendment all indicate that our rights preexist the

Constitution. But never mind the preamble, the Declaration, and the Ninth Amendment. Let's not appeal to any authority beyond our own common sense. Let's grant for argument's sake that the Constitution deserves veneration in ways analogous to our veneration of God.

Let's assume that the Constitution made us a nation and that it is the source of our rights. Then let's notice that the Constitution speaks for "We the People." Now combine these thoughts: if the Constitution made us as a people, and if the Constitution speaks for us as a people, it follows that we made ourselves a people and that we are the source of our rights. We the People decide the biggest questions for ourselves: who and what we are; what's good for us; what rights we have; how we should treat each other. Since the Constitution declares our voice the "supreme Law," we as a people answer ultimately only to ourselves. Never mind higher authority, like God or nature; never mind the dissenting individual, for whom the Constitution provides in several ways and who implicitly appeals to higher authority of one form or another; and never mind the rest of the "candid world" to which Jefferson and his confederates once gave reasons for declaring the nation's independence.

Revering the Constitution thus turns out to be a form of self-worship, and the big problem with self-worship is that it doesn't work. Not for us, at least. It doesn't work to secure a people's well-being in a world not of human making and beyond human control. Some politicians and some intellectuals will say things to the effect that we do make our own reality. No one really believes this, however. We can cope with reality, of course, changing things to our liking temporarily and at the retail level. But coping is not making, and retail is not wholesale. If we really could make our own reality our success would follow upon the mere declaration of it, and failure would be impossible. Indeed, failure would be inconceivable; we'd have no concept of it. We wouldn't labor for results because we wouldn't have to labor for results. We'd just go around saying (for no reason, since we'd have no needs) "let it be," as God created the world by saying, let it be. Although we creators might see our animated creations falling short of what they might call "their ends," we wouldn't count their falling short as "failure" if we made them (for our amusement?) to fall short. Their view of their nature and situation might include notions like action, choice, agency, and failure; but we, the makers, would know these notions to be illusions. If we could make our own reality the Constitution would be a good constitution and we'd be happy (boredom aside?) solely by proclamation. If we could make our own reality we'd see America's present situation as a case of national masochism, explicable by some theory of "different strokes." Suffice to say that if we have made our own reality, the reality that we've made includes a reality beyond our making, and beyond our control.

There would also be the problem of whom the word "we" included. Who would be the "we" who decided what's good and right for ourselves? The Reconstruction Congress and the U.S. Army tried to settle this question for the country in 1868 when they forced the Southern states to ratify the Fourteenth Amendment. This amendment makes all native-born and naturalized persons members of the constituent we, regardless of race, parentage, religion, or wealth. This, at any rate, is the constitutional part of the answer to who we might be. This constitutional answer would not only have a force of its own, it would register in any scientific answer. The social-scientific finding that segments of the population felt politically disfranchised would be visible partly in light of the legal-moral fact that it ought to be otherwise. Of course, for much of the nation's history—a shocking three-quarters to date—it was otherwise. For much of the nation's history, law-abiding and socially productive parts of the adult population were excluded from the constituent we, despite the creed that none should be governed without their consent. The nation's history thus shows that the identity of the constituent we is itself a political problem, even the biggest political problem. It makes no sense, therefore, to say that we decide the biggest questions; for with no prior agreement on the biggest questions, there is no we.

The American constitutional text supposes a preexisting community whose members aspire above all else to public goods like the common defense and the general welfare. The text is written as if these goods are real goods, goods that naturally attract competing conceptions. Articles I, V, and VII indicate by their provision for deliberative institutions that the best versions of these goods and the means thereto will be pursued through a continuing process of public reason. By banning titles of nobility and religious tests for national office, Articles I and VI indicate that the evidence supporting policy choices will be accessible in principle to people generally, not solely to any special generation, bloodline, or divinely privileged calling or group.

Agreement in these things—what and who we are, what we want most, how to find the best conceptions of what we want most, the best means thereto, and what counts as evidence in such matters—agreement in these things wouldn't be everything, but it would be a whole lot—enough to keep things going. Disagreement in these things was enough to cause one civil war and may yet cause another. Agreement in these things depends altogether on the attractiveness of real goods, goods not of our making, preambular goods like justice and the general welfare that stand proudly on their own, without apologetic quotation marks. By implicitly denying the existence of such goods, constitution worshippers leave nothing for competing conceptions of an idea to get closer to. Competing conceptions are no longer versions of general ideas in whose light some conceptions are better than others; they're just competing conceptions, period. You have your view of "Justice," I have mine, and there's no truth of the matter for us jointly to strive for and embrace at the expense of our initial opinions. With nothing to get closer to, deliberation degenerates from a truth-seeking process to a bargaining process. But bargaining for personal advantage, even bargaining in good faith, in the manner of "enlightened" self-servers, is no substitute for deliberating about truth. Bargainers as such support the practice of good-faith bargaining only to the extent that its payoff to them personally is more likely and more attractive than that of other processes. When bargainers come to believe that processes like fraud and violence are sure to pay more, they may continue bargaining from habit, but they can see no reason for bargaining. Reduce real goods to apparent goods and deny that (as the preamble and Article V indicate) the quest by fallible actors for real goods is foundational to the national community, and there can be no unconditional reason to prefer bargaining over fraud and violence.

Constitution worship thus indicates that force is the ultimate source of what's good and right—the source, rather, of what's called good and right. This downward spiral from Constitution worship to moral skepticism and ultimately force makes constitution worship a bad idea. And it is altogether incompatible with the framers' idea that the chief function of the American Constitution is reconciling public opinion to objective standards of the public interest and political morality.

Why Venerating the Founding Can Be a Good Idea

Venerating the Constitution is a bad idea because it obscures the inevitability of constitutional failure and the corresponding need to promote reformist institutions and foster reformist virtues. Venerating the Constitution can be a good idea when failure is irreversible and illusion is the way to keep a dying nation comfortable for as long as possible. Venerating the Founding (not the Constitution) is different, actually quite different.

A constitution in the American sense is a legally obligatory arrangement of offices, powers, and rights written out on paper or parchment. Founding of a constitution, on the other hand, is a kind of action. This kind of action has its own preconditions, stages, agents, and subjects; it also requires its own competences and virtues. To venerate the Founding we would venerate the crafting and ratification of a set of means for ends external and superior to the means crafted. This understanding of a founding act is preserved in the Constitution's preamble, which declares the document established for the sake of ends such as the common defense, the general welfare, and the blessings of liberty. As a matter of practical reason, ends are superior to means. From a framer's view, the common defense and the general welfare are superior to institutions established to pursue those ends. Madison affirms the superiority of ends to institutional means when he says in *Federalist* 45 that "the real welfare of the . . . people, is the supreme object to be pursued; and . . . no form of government whatever has any other value than as it may be fitted for the attainment of this object." Madison seemed dead serious about this principle. He applied it to the proposal of the Philadelphia Convention and to the Union itself. "Were the plan of the convention adverse to the public happiness," he said in *Federalist* 45, "my voice would be, reject the plan. Were the Union itself inconsistent with the public happiness, it would be, Abolish the Union" (45:309)—the very Union, mind you, that the preamble and Article XIII of the Articles of Confederation declared to be "perpetual." Thus, to venerate the Founding is to revisit a perspective in which the Constitution is both a mere proposal and a mere set of means. To commemorate the Founding is to recall a point of view in which the Constitution is not the most important thing and where fidelity to law is no substitute for public-spiritedness, deliberation, leadership, and trust. Better, I submit, to venerate the Founding than the Constitution.

But this conclusion needs refinement. We should venerate the Founding and the framers, but only in the service of a larger good. Were our admiration focused on a particular act and particular actors, the reason would lie in the excellence of their particular product, which, like all manmade constitutions, is at best a contingent and potentially failed instrument of its ends. If there's lasting, noncontingent value in venerating our framers and our founding it lies not in who they might have been but in what they aspired to demonstrate, namely, humanity's capacity for "establishing good government from reflection and choice." They made and remade constitutions, we're sprung from them, maybe we can emulate them, when the time comes, as it has come. Venerating the framers and their act makes sense if they can realistically serve as a model for our own conduct.

This position may open me to the charge of lawlessness, ingratitude, and even impiety—sins against a document and a system that we, actually or virtually, are sworn to preserve and pass to the future.[10] So permit me a brief defense against this charge. First a quick review: I've argued that we should commemorate the Founding, not the Constitution, and I've argued for commemorating the Founding for the virtues it represents, not for the constitution it produced. My argument so far has been an argument from the possibility of constitutional failure, a possibility no one can deny. I've argued elsewhere to the same conclusion from the nature of the people's welfare, which Madison says in *Federalist* 45 is the supreme object of any good government, regardless of form.[11] Arguments from the possibility of failure and from the nature of human welfare appeal to goods higher than the positive law. Because American systems of law are expressly established to pursue these goods, laws disconnected from reasonable versions of these goods aren't really laws, aren't really *constitutional* laws.

Though this instrumentalist attitude toward law reflects traditional doctrine, some will call it a formula for chaos, and I concede it may well be. Better, you might say, some authority, however flawed, than none at all. I respect the point. Appeals to higher authority or, as I prefer, true authority, have led to death and destruction in the past. So let me try a different tack. Let me try to defend venerating constitution makers and their virtues by appealing not to higher values but to the law itself, to the Constitution itself.

Assume that we all take an oath to preserve and defend the Constitution. Many of us have taken the oath in good faith, as have our representatives in all parts of our governments. Our question now is whether the oath favors the Constitution and the historical act that established it more than the virtues that the American founding aspired to represent. Here again, we can't venerate both at the same time, for a constitution that worked perfectly would eliminate the need for further acts of constitution making and reform, and celebrating virtues associated with constitution making and reform would be both pointless and subversive of a good government. Why remind people of things that aren't needed anymore and whose revival might be harmful? So, our question: does the oath to preserve and defend the Constitution elevate *this* constitution and *its* founding over mankind's capacity to establish good government from reflection and choice?

Swearing to preserve and defend the Constitution is not promising to leave it as is, for the Constitution itself provides for change in Article V. By providing for amendments, Article V implies that the Constitution may need amending. Article V thus bestows on the Constitution a specific property, the property of amendability. The amendability of this constitution and therewith the opportunity and the right to redo our founding is thus made part of what we take an oath to preserve and defend. Our constitution is thus officially "open to thought"—that is, open to reasoned criticism and change. Let's think about this a bit further.

In view of Article V, we're under an obligation to preserve and defend almost no part of our existing constitution because almost every part is amendable. This includes Article V itself. We can reconsider Article V, and we will surely have to do so eventually, for Article V has insuperable problems. Article V purports to put equal suffrage of the states in the Senate virtually beyond amendment by permitting change only on the consent of each state. In addition, three-quarters of the states are most unlikely ever to make the Constitution easier to amend than it presently is. These virtually unamendable provisions of Article V are virtually closed to thought—closed to reasoned reconsideration. And because they are closed to rethinking, they offend the principle of amendability itself, the very thing that Article V is supposed to embody. Article V is thus at war with itself; it represents a principle that it defeats in practice. This isn't a problem unique to Article V; under the right circumstances any process or rule can defeat the purpose it was designed to serve. Under the right circumstances (or the wrong ones) a rule can be at war with the principle that justifies it. Yet this is a special problem for an amending rule, which is supposed to provide for the defect of rules generally. If and when a constitution's amending rule becomes unworkable or unworkable in a timely way, the rule ceases to be what the constitution says it is: part of a larger scheme for pursuing real goods. It ceases to be an amending rule because it doesn't work and can't be made to work as an amending rule.

Americans have faced this situation before. The framers of our present constitution encountered an unworkable amending rule in Article XIII of the Articles of Confederation. Here was a rule that gave a bare majority of Rhode Island (1/60th of the nation's total population) a veto over everyone else, and past experience had shown Rhode Island's willingness to use the veto. Madison was clear in *Federalist* 40 about the only rational course in this circumstance: ignore the old rule, submit a new rule to the people, and let them accept or reject the new rule as they choose to act on it or not. Quoting from the Declaration of Independence and citing the nation's revolutionary experience with unauthorized committees, congresses, and constitutional conventions, Madison said that "in all great changes of established governments, forms ought to give way to substance" lest the "transcendent and precious right of the people to 'abolish or alter their . . . to effect their safety and happiness'" be rendered "nominal and nugatory." Since the people can't "move in concert towards their object" in a spontaneous fashion, Madison added, "it is . . . essential that such changes be instituted by some informal and unauthorized propositions, made by some patriotic and respectable citizen or number of citizens" (40:265). The country evidently agreed. It ignored the old Article XIII and followed the new Article VII to establish the new Article V and the rest of the new constitution. And it did all this in the only way it could peacefully have done so: by following the lead of "some patriotic and respectable . . . number of citizens" and approving propositions that were "informal and unauthorized."

So, in my defense against the charge of lawlessness, I invoke the constitutional text that embodies the principle of amendability and the historic words and actions that honored that principle. Venerating the Founding as founding over both the Constitution and the Constitution's founding would therefore be no lawless act. Nor would it violate the constitutional oath. The Constitution itself, as written, together with the actions that produced it and the tradition that justifies it—all these things display a principle of amendability. As a logical matter, this principle of amendability cannot be captured by any sort of rule. It points ultimately not to a set of rules but to an attitudinal situation. As Madison indicated, in *Federalist* 40, it points to a competent and patriotic leadership community that enjoys the public's trust. The nation's "openness to thought"—the possibility in America of government "by reflection and choice"—depends on this ensemble of virtues and actors. So does the Constitution's survival.

The Plan of This Book

If we have good reason to talk about constitutional failure, what, exactly, are we talking about? What questions do we ask in deciding whether or to what extent the Constitution is failing? Chapter 2 of this book will show how different answers to this question reflect three different views of the Constitution's central purpose: either to protect rights, or to provide processes of democratic choice, or to pursue the ends listed in the preamble. Chapter 2 reiterates my argument in other places that while the Constitution was designed to perform all three functions, its *chief* function is to pursue preambular ends conceived as a set of substantive social conditions, such as peace and prosperity. Chapter 3 takes a closer look at the substantive social ends discussed in chapter 2 and applies principles of practical reason to any specification of constitutional ends to conclude that the one unquestionable constitutional end is a secular public reasonableness as the attitude of Americans taken at random. I call the political manifestation of this secular public reasonableness a "healthy politics," and upon describing this state of affairs I conclude that maintaining a healthy politics is essential to constitutional success. I conclude also that the chronic absence of a healthy politics is one form—the crucial form—of constitutional failure. This "attitudinal" test of constitutional failure is the answer to those who think that because American institutions are intact the American Constitution still works, even if American politics is sick. My contention is that sick politics is the decisive sign of a bad constitution and that incurably sick politics proves constitutional failure, even if (as presently) the dead man still walks.

Chapter 4 applies the central finding of the preceding chapter— constitutional failure as a matter of attitude—to Madison's belief that checks and balances can serve as a substitute for virtue—a substitute for what Madison believed to be, and what I'll argue must be, a government by a trusted and trustworthy elite. The chapter situates Madison between classical and modernist traditions about the need for virtuous political leadership and shows that the ancients were right. Though Madison himself deemphasized the need for virtue in *The Federalist*, he effectively conceded the tradi-tion's greater wisdom when, both in the Constitutional Conven-tion and later as president, he called for a national university as the font of a national leadership community. Chapter 5 returns to the implications of the Constitution's preamble to elaborate and defend Walter Murphy's proposal that the preeminent constitu-tional virtue is not fidelity to an existing constitution but the ca-pacity for constitutional reform. Chapter 5 discusses developments in America's political and intellectual cultures, from the rise of the religious right and free-market absolutism to academic value-skepticism, that defeat realistic hopes for a healthy politics and the prospects for constitutional reform. The chapter argues that what little hope remains depends almost entirely on chance. Hope rests also on constitutional studies programs in a dwindling hand-ful of the nation's universities, notwithstanding the fact that some of these programs have been captured or are being captured by the hard ideological right. Though the Constitution's prospects are at best poor, the concluding chapter, like the book as a whole, assumes that, in the right circumstances, accurate diagnosis can be a step toward cure and that the right circumstances may chance again.

2

Failure at What Kind of Thing?

Talk of constitutional failure presupposes some idea of constitutional success. This chapter discusses the general kind of thing the Constitution is supposed to accomplish. I argue that the Constitution envisions more than a government that proceeds fairly and respects rights. It envisions what its preamble says it envisions: a good state of society, good things like national security ("the common defence") and a prosperous people ("the general Welfare"). Honoring constitutional rights and observing fair procedures are part of the picture; some constitutional rights and processes may even be integral to the goods sought, as property (a set of government-secured rights) is integral to prosperity (a social state of affairs), and weighing diverse views (hence, free speech) can lead to better conceptions of prosperity. But exemptions from power (constitutional rights) and the procedures through which power is exercised (constitutional structures) are at best either elements or derivatives of the ends of government and in any case subordinate to the ends of government—the public purposes that the framers had in mind and that we all have in mind and must have in mind for the collective act of establishing a government to make sense.

In the chapter that follows this one I move beyond the nature of constitutional ends (the kind of thing they are, namely, public purposes) to a concrete account of these ends. They initially appear to be economic growth, economic fairness, and other features of "the Large Commercial Republic" that Martin Diamond derived from *The Federalist* some fifty years ago. Yet the Large Commercial Republic proves to be no more than a conception of the good life for Americans, and conceptions of ends like the common defense and the general welfare can be wrong, especially as circumstances change. General ideas like the common defense and the general welfare also attract competing conceptions. Thus, economic growth might compete with spiritual growth as the best understanding of well-being. Yet government as a voluntary human institution would make no sense unless some conceptions of security, well-being, and the like were truly better than others. Upon reflection, the highest attainable constitutional end turns out to be the reasonable pursuit of constitutional ends—reasonable debate about what they mean in practice and how to realize them. This reasonable pursuit is the defining practice of an attitudinal state of affairs. The preconditions of this state of affairs justify calling it a "secular public reasonableness." I call the general diffusion of this "secular public reasonableness" a "healthy politics," to be contrasted with the sick politics of America today. I argue in this chapter that chronic failure to maintain a healthy politics is a sure sign of constitutional failure, even if a sick political culture could somehow manage to honor constitutional rights and observe constitutional forms.

A healthy politics seems initially to be a kind of process whose

participants have rights of equal representation and expression, and
it is all that. Maybe, as the framers concluded, a healthy politics
also depends on the diversion of human energies from sectarian
and other noneconomic ends to negotiable economic ends. We
shall see, however, that participants in a healthy politics must see
themselves as contributing in some way to a quest for a true understanding of real public goods. Because the Declaration of Independence and the Constitution indicate that these real goods warrant
sacrifices of life and fortune, the ends in question must be worth
more than economic rights, economic ends, and the processes of
compromising economic ends. Though, I submit, this is no partisan conclusion in terms of how it was reached, I acknowledge that,
under present circumstances, it has a partisan bite. It counsels cau-
tion in seeking political leadership either from the nation's business
community (committed to return on investment and, at best, to the
Large Commercial Republic) or from those intellectuals who treat
an expanding domestic product (never mind its distribution) as a
sign of political truth. Readers might also be prepared for offenses
to their democratic sensibilities. Some might object to my emphasis on the need for political leadership. I remind them of Madison's
statement in *Federalist* 57 that the test of a constitution is its reli-
able production of good leaders (57:384). I also recall Hamilton's
conception of leadership in *Federalist* 71 as educating the public
to its true interest, against its unreflective inclinations, if need be
(71:482–483). Though these tenets of the old Federalist Party may
suggest an undemocratic elitism, they can as easily suggest faith
in democracy's ability to generate competent and public-spirited
leadership. And the current state of American politics and government puts the burden on observers who somehow still believe that
a populist version of American democracy can work.

How General Theories of the Constitution Affect the Meaning of Constitutional Failure

The American Constitution is a collection of different kinds of norms. This collection includes: ends or goods listed in the Constitution's preamble; a list of authorizations or powers, mostly in Article I, Section 8; exemptions from authorizations or powers, listed mostly in the Bill of Rights and the Civil War Amendments; provisions for offices, functions, and personnel in Articles I, II, and III ("constitutional structures"); and provision for constitutional change in the amending rules of Article V. All general understandings of the Constitution contain or imply theories of each of these types of provision. Yet understandings of the Constitution differ by their ranking of these several provisions. Though a positive or ends-oriented view of the Constitution has a place for constitutional rights and constitutional structures, it views preambular ends as fundamental, the point of the enterprise, and it construes constitutional powers broadly to facilitate the pursuit of constitutional ends. By contrast, though a negative or rights-oriented view of the Constitution has a place for constitutional structures and powers, it views constitutional powers narrowly as needed to protect constitutional rights. This section discusses three or four different understandings of the Constitution as a whole: positive constitutionalism, negative constitutionalism, process constitutionalism, and a form of process constitutionalism that is actually a form of positive constitutionalism. I try to show how these different understandings of the Constitution shape conceptions of constitutional success and failure, and I argue for the superiority of a positive or ends-oriented constitutionalism.

The Positive, Ends-Oriented, or Instrumental Constitution

A general theory of the Constitution will have its corollary view of constitutional success and constitutional failure. Positive constitutionalism originates in the Declaration of Independence, specifically, in the claim that "the People" have a natural right to abolish old governments and establish new ones "as to them shall seem most likely to effect their Safety and Happiness." The constitutional text expresses this instrumental view when it says the people ordain a government to pursue the public goods listed in the preamble. Instrumentalist thought pervades *The Federalist*. This most famous but often misunderstood defense of the Constitution promises a government that will secure the people's liberty, dignity, and happiness (1:6, 7). It holds not chiefly for "limited government" but for strong government, "the supreme object" of which is "the real welfare of the great body of the people" (45:309).[1] Instrumentalism describes a founding generation not in thrall to some ideology but determined to remedy the old Congress's inability to secure specific national needs, such as foreign and domestic credit (threatened by America's failure to repay the revolutionary war debt); shipping on the Mississippi and trade with the West Indies (blocked, respectively, by Spain and England, who feared no effective response from people who wouldn't pay for a credible military force); and threats to a national market and investor confidence (from the states' trade barriers, debtor-relief laws, and paper-money laws).[2] Because supplying needs is normally conceived as a good thing, and because defenders of the proposed government claimed that it would supply these needs, they conceived the new government not as a necessary evil but as a good thing. In a comment whose relevance is depressingly obvious in what remains in key respects the Age of Reagan, *Federalist* 1 says that "a dangerous ambition more often lurks behind the specious mask of zeal for the rights of the people than under the forbidding appearance of zeal for the firmness and efficiency of government" (1:6).

In addition to historical authorities like *The Federalist* and the Declaration of Independence, common sense supports an ends-oriented view of the Constitution. Because no mentally sound persons would establish a coercive power over themselves just to limit that power (If limiting government is the sole or chief object, why establish government in the first place?) or to watch it operate (Coercive power is not a performing art, a spectator sport, or a thing of beauty to behold.), the establishment of a government must be seen as a means to positive goods, like national security and prosperity, goods that can't be approximated without government. True, democratic politics (governing and being governed in turn) may ennoble a people, but it will do so only if it is a source of long-term goods like the security and prosperity of the community at large. These background tenets of common sense are embodied in the Constitution's preamble. They enable us to recognize the relevance and normative force of the argument of *The Federalist* and the stated purposes of those responsible for the constitutional revolution of 1787.[3]

The Negative or Rights-Oriented Constitution

Next comes the negative-liberties view of the Constitution as a whole. This view flows from a distrust of government and gives pride of place to constitutional rights. It holds that men entered civil society from a state of nature in order to protect private rights.

It sees the Constitution's chief function as limiting government in behalf of private rights. The Constitution thus becomes a "charter of negative liberties": as such, it guarantees exemptions *from* governmental power; it does not promise governmental benefits or the pursuit of public goods. Government is of course expected to provide benefits, like police protection from private violence, but it isn't constitutionally obligated to provide any benefits. To the negative constitutionalist, the provision of benefits is a matter of discretionary public choice, not constitutional imperative. By this model a constitution fails when the government it establishes enters into a long-term and irreversible pattern of violating private rights. This theory would regard the "welfare state" as an example of constitutional failure since such a state would redistribute property from those who have earned it to those who haven't earned it, thus violating the reason men established government in the first place: to secure their property.

Negative constitutionalism is so patently indefensible that one can hold it only contingently, as it happens to serve one's immediate interests, and only insofar as it serves one's immediate interests. By its inability to account for the Constitution as the product of a human act, it threatens constitutionalism itself—the idea that a people can form and reform governments "to effect their Safety and Happiness." Because common sense knows, and moral philosophy has known at least since Aristotle, that people act for what they think is some good, we know that no mentally sound actors would establish a government for the chief purpose of limiting it or if they expected more harm than good from it. Nor could reason comprehend establishing a government to pursue public goods without obligating it to do so. In addition, negative constitutionalism ignores classical liberal theorists who describe the motivation for establishing government as the protection of private rights *not* against the government, but against private parties. Vindicating rights against government can't be a reason for leaving the state of nature because there is no government in a state of nature. Negative constitutionalism also ignores the fact that rights don't protect rights; power protects rights—the state's coercive power protects private rights from private assault.

In denominating rights "negative liberties," negative constitutionalism ignores the fact that the value of rights depends on the goods that the rights are rights to and that violating rights doesn't affect the rights, it affects possession or enjoyment of these goods. A victim of theft is deprived of a thing that she has property in, which thing is a positive good; she is not deprived of the *right* to that thing. She retains the right after she's lost the thing, even if she's lost the thing partly through a fault of her own, like her gullibility or lack of vigilance. She couldn't ask the government to restore her enjoyment of the thing or compensate for its loss if she had no continuing right to the thing and if the state lacked the authority to remedy her loss. And her appeal to the state would assume much more than the state's authority to help her. It would assume the resources to help her, resources collected and deployed by the powers to tax and spend.

Regarding the powers to tax and spend, the negative-liberties view ignores the fact that the state that vindicates private rights is a redistributive state: it acts for the common good on resources extracted from those who have enough to be taxed. It redistributes also when its system of criminal justice (comprised of laws, police, prosecutors, courts, prisons) takes a form of property from the poor, namely, their natural right to preserve themselves as they deem necessary, even by helping themselves to the surplus property of others. Some might contend that the state takes nothing from the poor because the poor (somehow) consented to be deprived of their natural right of self-help. But, again, people act only for the sake of what they think is good, consent is a form of action, and therefore people could have consented only to governments likely to improve their condition, not worsen it. Classical liberal theory does promise that all responsible persons will be better off if they abandon self-help. Yet the criminal law applies to all, even to those whose prospects might be objectively hopeless. The emergence of such a class in America and elsewhere becomes increasingly more likely as the income gap grows and upward mobility declines worldwide. It thus becomes increasingly harder to deny that the modern state redistributes property from the worse-off to the better-off, and increasingly more hypocritical for the well-off to complain about the "redistributive state."

As weak as the negative-liberties view is, it is no straw man; it is the official position of the U.S. Supreme Court, which presently denies that government has the least affirmative duty of the night watchman state: protecting helpless children from predictable physical violence. Led by Chief Justice William Rehnquist, a 5:4 court reached this startling result in the veritable emblem of negative constitutionalism, *DeShaney v. Winnebago* (1989).[4] This case involved a four-year old boy whose father beat him into a permanent vegetative state. The Court held that a county welfare agency had no constitutional duty to protect the boy, even though the agency had monitored the child's situation for two years and even though local ER physicians had informed the agency of violence against the child on three separate occasions. As a general matter, said the chief justice, the states have no federal constitutional duty "to provide substantive services" for their people (ibid.,

196). The most likely explanation for this perverse proposition was the majority's wariness of any holding that would imply a duty to provide welfare services beyond such minima as police protection. Yet Rehnquist knew what he was doing. He correctly saw no principled line between police protection and broader benefits. With no principled distinction between tax-supported police protection and tax-supported protection against things like unwarranted poverty, and with a determination to deny the latter at all costs, Rehnquist denied a right to the former. In this way Rehnquist acknowledged that all governmental services are forms of welfare, and that recognizing a right to the least of such goods opens the door to much more—really, to all that government can provide or facilitate without doing more harm to its people than good.[5]

Unable to swallow Rehnquist's solution to their problem, other rightists have tried to recognize affirmative rights to the state's protection against fraud and violence without going all the way to state provision for the poor. Their theory is that protections against fraud and violence are not redistributive in nature because the taxpayers don't lose anything—the police and fire protection they receive has a value greater (or is more valuable to them) than the taxes they pay for those services. But this theory ill serves rightist aims, for who can deny that life in communities with wider prosperity, more upward mobility, and less crime and dependency might be worth paying for? If police and fire protection don't have to be seen as welfare, neither do programs like the GI Bill, Social Security, Head Start, school lunches, and food stamps. All can be seen as investments in the nation's future. Do adequately nourished children not have better chances to succeed in school and stay off welfare rolls as adults? And if, on the other hand, Social Security and the rest *must* be seen as welfare, so must police and fire protection, for all governmental activities require taxes that some people prefer to avoid and in fact work very hard and spend enormous amounts to avoid.[6]

True, some policies perpetuate dependency on government; but if dependency were always bad, dependency on the police would be bad, and the liberal state would make no sense. That some policies perpetuate avoidable dependencies serves only to indicate the debatable nature of any given policy. It does not justify a wholesale presumption against government—the presumptive priority of private rights over public purposes (the consumer over the citizen, the base over the noble) that defines negative constitutionalism.

Process Constitutionalism

Our final view of the Constitution can be called process or procedural constitutionalism. This view has been confounded with a commitment to democratic processes unconnected to substantive outcomes such as peace, prosperity, and fairness. Proceduralism unconnected to substantive commitments is a mistake because there's no such thing as an identifiable manmade procedure that's unconnected to a good of some sort, either ultimate or instrumental.[7] Process constitutionalism is therefore best seen as a kind of ends-oriented or positive view. In this view the Constitution is essentially a set of procedures for representing private interests and coordinating their pursuit, which system of representation and coordination of private interests is confounded with democracy.[8] This too is a mistake. If democracy is a good it is a public good, and if there are people who love it, they are willing to sacrifice their private interests (pay taxes, fight, forgo gain) for it. Democrats would either be public-spirited or self-regarding in a way that sought the approval of their communities, which would make them practically public-spirited. As genuine lovers of democracy, democrats would want democracy—democracy itself, not necessarily democracy as they conceived it. (If they wanted their conception of democracy just because it was their conception, they would love themselves, not democracy.[9]) True democrats would thus seek the best conception of democracy and value the preconditions of such a quest, which would include substantive commitments associated with a range of freedoms essential to the quest for truth against the often false security of conventional opinion.

These substantive commitments would in turn range beyond freedoms of inquiry, due process, and property to a general secular reasonableness—a habit of acting toward others only for reasons that people generally can appreciate as good reasons. I have called this a *secular* reasonableness because it precludes reasons based on private revelations or evidence not shared or sharable in principle by people generally, like the evidence of Jesus's divinity to which Martin Luther said God's curse had closed the minds of Jews.[10] Though this secular reasonableness might embrace economic commitments that channeled people's energies away from sectarian commitments that favor scriptural or clerical authority over science, it would also preclude an axiomatic materialism that closed itself to reason's limitations and the case for religion's role in a civilized life. If the best conception of democracy should be found to include conditions like equal opportunity and upward mobility, committed democrats would willingly pay the taxes and fight the wars needed to secure these conditions. (The American Civil War was such a war; America's current culture war may prove to be another.) If democracy involved informed citizen participation in politics, democrats would pay the many costs needed to acquire the requisite knowledge. Because democrats would be public-spirited (or self-regarding in a way practically indistinguishable from public spiritedness) they would want to do the right thing by others, not what they might think is the right thing, and their resulting sense of fallibility would make them value a regime of good-faith deliberation, as opposed to a regime of self-serving bargaining.

The process view of the Constitution presupposes a person far different from the true democrat. The process view assumes a person who is interested in his private advantage, not the public interest. For him constitutional processes are ultimately means for pursuing his private wants in a manner that enables him to live with others who, like him, are moved chiefly by their private wants. For him the "ends of government" are not public purposes but his private purposes. If he could acknowledge a public purpose it would be the coordination of diverse private wants—that is, those diverse private wants that can be coordinated. He would treat as punishable crimes acts that flowed from private wants that fell outside this range. He could come to value this coordination of amenable private wants, but only from habit (not rational conviction) and as a condition for pursuing his private wants. Should he be able to get away with pursuing wants outside the permissible range of wants, he would have a reason to do so and no reason not to, for he recognizes no public reason that doesn't serve his private wants and serve them optimally. Because this person conflates the good with whatever he might happen to desire—collapses the normative distance between what's good and what he thinks is good—he knows what's good because he knows what he desires. This makes him a bargainer, at best a compromiser. He can have doubts about means, and therefore he can deliberate about them. But he has no concept of deliberation about ends.

The process view of the Constitution faces two insuperable difficulties. First, it implicitly reduces the language of the Constitution to window dressing, for that language assumes individuals who see themselves as parts of a collective (a "We the People") and who are sufficiently devoted to public purposes to install coercive authority over their private pursuits. The self-regarding actor of process constitutionalism simply can't understand or empathize with the opening appeal of *The Federalist* to its readers' philanthropy and patriotism. Indeed, the self-regarding actor can fully subscribe to no normative principle of general applicability. A case in point involves the Declaration of Independence. Some who said all men were created equal did so solely because it served their momentary interest to say so; they proved by their continuing commitment to slavery that they didn't really mean it.

Nor can the process constitutionalist accept the Constitution as supreme law, for his obedience to law is contingent on whether, all things considered, it provides an optimal course to the satisfaction of his private wants. If he wants something badly enough to risk criminal sanctions, he has every reason to pursue it and no reason not to. For by "reason" he means a private good—a reason he can give to himself privately, not publicly to others, and not to himself as another. Reasons he gives to others count as mere rationalizations for his private reasons. The process constitutionalist can thus have no normative theory of legal obligation. He can't give himself a reason for obeying the law when the balance of his personal wants and aversions indicates disobedience. Consenting to the law's supremacy could not be a reason for the purely self-regarding actor even if he had (somehow) consented to the law. For a regime of promise-keeping is a public good (integral to democracy), promises are made to others, and if kept just because promised, kept from respect for others. To the extent that a self-regarding actor kept his promises to others at a permanent cost to himself, he wouldn't be a self-regarding actor.

A theory of the Constitution that implicitly dismisses its language as meaningless and denies its claim to supremacy is at best an anthropological theory *about* the Constitution, explaining its origin and history. It would not be a normative theory *of* the Constitution, a theory for persons who had reason to follow, preserve, and defend the Constitution.

How Kinds of Instrumentalism Differ

To this last observation the process theorist can respond that he's not alone—that a positive constitutionalist also has problems with the Constitution's declaration of supremacy. Positive constitutionalists are ends-oriented; they see constitutional authorizations as means to preambular ends. As an abstract matter of practical reason, means have only contingent value. Their value ceases when they no longer work. The framers themselves evinced this attitude toward means when they ignored the supreme law of their day and proposed ratification of the new constitution by procedures contrary to those of the existing constitution. Madison openly embraced an instrumental logic in *Federalist* 40 when he condemned Article XIII of the Articles of Confederation, which gave each of the thirteen states a veto over the rest. Adhering to Article XIII would have permitted "a majority of 1/60th of the people of America" (the population of Rhode Island, which refused to send delegates to the Federal Convention) to veto the will of as many as "59-60ths of the people." And that, he said, would have been an "absurdity" (40:263). Madison went on to generalize the point:

"[I]n all great changes of established governments, forms ought to give way to substance . . . [because] a rigid adherence in such cases to the former, would render nominal and nugatory, the transcendent and precious right of the people to 'abolish or alter their governments as to them hall seem most likely to effect their safety and happiness' . . . [and that] since it is impossible for the people spontaneously and universally, to move in concert toward their object . . . it is therefore essential, that such changes be instituted by some *informal and unauthorized propositions,* made by some respectable citizen or number of citizens" (40:265, his emphasis). Our process theorist might make the most of this passage. Are "informal and unauthorized propositions" not euphemistic of "lawless and unauthorized propositions"? How, if at all, does the instrumentalism of process constitutionalism differ from the instrumentalism of positive constitutionalism?

To see the difference, consider the Supreme Court's decision in *Employment Division v. Smith* (1990).[11] *Smith* holds that if a state (Oregon, in this case) wants to outlaw use of peyote (a mild hallucinogen) as a threat to the public health or for other secular reasons, it may do so without regard for the Native American religious rites in which peyote is used. *Smith* holds more generally that believers can't claim religious exemptions from broadly applicable laws that are designed to serve secular purposes. *Smith* outraged believers and their supporters in the civil liberties community. They charged that in spite of the Constitution's guarantee of freedom of religious exercise, *Smith* forced believers to disregard their religious duties for no compelling reason on the part of the states. For argument's sake, let's accept this assessment of *Smith.* In that event, the decision could have flowed from a hostility to religion in general or to the Native American religion of the respondents in the case. This would have been the "reason" of the purely self-regarding actor of process constitutional theory. I put "reason" in scare quotes here because, without more, hostility either to religion or to a specific religion could only *explain* the decision; it could not *justify* it, at least not in an American court.

But *Smith* might also have represented an honest commitment to the Constitution—even if *Smith* effectively repealed the Free Exercise Clause. After all, Justice Antonin Scalia had a point in *Smith*: every man would indeed be "a law unto himself" if one's religious beliefs could justify disobedience to generally applicable laws enacted for secular purposes. Such was the Oregon statute at issue in *Smith*; no evidence indicated that hostility toward Native Americans motivated the law's ban on peyote. Justice Scalia may thus have considered the Free Exercise Clause a mistake, perhaps an unnecessary duplication of the Establishment Clause, which prohibits laws whose purpose is either to advance or to burden particular religions or religion in general. Weakening the Free Exercise Clause did not necessarily signal fidelity to one's prejudices over fidelity to the law; it may have meant fidelity to the law's broader purposes, all of which are secular purposes. In this connection one could note the absence of religious aims in the preamble and the ban on religious tests for offices in Article VI. To the claim that the Free Exercise Clause elevates religious practice to preambular status (a blessing of liberty?), one could reply that the Free Exercise Clause is an amendment to the Constitution, that Article V calls amendments "part[s]" of the Constitution, and that practical reason shapes parts to fit wholes and thus subordinates parts to wholes. One could also say that the amending provision of Article V implies constitutional fallibility, that fallibility admits the possibility of constitutional mistakes, and that constitutional mistakes

have happened before and been remedied before by means beyond
Article V. (Were the Civil War Amendments voluntarily ratified?
Did Appomattox not doom the Fugitive Slave Clause even without
the Thirteenth Amendment?)

Here, then, would be the difference between disobeying the
law from the self-regarding perspective of process constitutionalism and the ends-orientation of the positive constitutionalist: the
latter alone can offer a public justification in terms of the law's
own aims. The latter alone can claim with a straight face that his
course is lawful in the deeper sense of reasonable and that the contrary course is actually unlawful because manifestly absurd. Would
allowing uninhibited claims of religious exemptions from secular
laws not destroy civil society? Who would have let Abraham sacrifice Isaac because Abraham believed God commanded it? Many
of us firmly believe the story told in Genesis 22. Yet what believer
among us would support a law that permitted private revelations to
exempt individuals from laws against murder and other proscrip-
tions of the criminal law? Until some prominent sector of American opinion dares openly to construe the Free Exercise Clause to
that effect, one can doubt that any Americans take the Free Exercise Clause seriously—certainly not seriously enough for costs of
biblical proportions.

About Rights and Institutions

The ends-orientation of constitutional language and *The Federalist*
turns out to be the only view of the Constitution that makes practical sense. This makes constitutional failure the failure to achieve,
maintain, or progress toward the ends of the preamble, and the
question of constitutional failure would involve issues of means

(what works; what's affordable?) and ends (what's best, or the best that we're capable of?). Since honoring rights and structures may be integral to progress toward preambular ends, constitutional failure could also involve the breakdown of constitutional institutions and the chronic violation of constitutional rights. But the Constitution would remain an instrument of its ends, and the test of its failure or success would remain a preambular test. The specifics of such a test will occupy us in chapter 3. Yet the firm grip of negative and procedural constitutionalism on American thought necessitates additional observations about constitutional rights and institutions.

Regarding institutions, several logical points should suffice. Constitutional institutions are means to ends of some sort, either public purposes, private purposes, or both. Means that don't work aren't really means. And when means that are declared law don't work, ignoring them can be consistent with the law's purposes. The American founding is a case in point. Congress instructed the Constitutional Convention to amend the Articles of Confederation in ways that would make the government adequate to the exigencies of the union. The framers acted according to this charge when they ignored Article XIII, the amending rule of the Articles, for an amending rule that makes amendments virtually impossible isn't really an amending rule; it doesn't do the work that defines rules of its kind. Article XIII may have been an ersatz amending rule, but an ersatz rule is no more a rule than an ersatz chair is a chair. An amending procedure must be a real amending procedure, just as a chair must be a real chair. Any claim that Article XIII was an amending procedure is disconnected from the realities of life with which manmade constitutions are designed to cope.

To those who say this observation is inapt when applied to Article XIII because the fault lay with Rhode Island, not Article XIII, I answer that a rule is always more than a rule. Rules are always rules for someone or for some types of actors for the accomplishment of some purpose. Amending rules of particular constitutions are addressed to specific populations as ways to amend. Article XIII was thus the rule for Americans who lived under the Articles to use for amending the Articles. But Article XIII wasn't really that because it didn't work for Americans who lived under the Articles. The same applies to the Constitution as a whole. It is what it says it is: a scheme for the American people steadily to improve their condition as needed for progress toward preambular ends. When the condition of this people begins to decline, there is evidence that Article V isn't working for the people it is supposed to work for. Their condition declines; they need change to arrest the decline; yet change isn't happening. Needed change that isn't happening indicates institutional failure. The test of institutions is concrete social results. No results and no reasonable prospects for results means no obligation to obey, for the law was ratified as an instrument, the law therefore is a law-as-instrument, and the law-as-instrument has ceased to exist. Constitutional logic compels the conclusion of no obligation when the law has ceased to work, and in *Federalist* 40 Madison affirmed this logic for his generation.

This needn't mean that all institutions are defeasible. It does mean that all formal institutions are defeasible. Institutions that are not defeasible are those deeply entrenched, perhaps even natural, institutions that may constitute our very identity as human beings. I mean primarily the institutions of language, logic, and the evidentiary maxims and protocols (e.g., "seeing is believing,") associated with demonstration and persuasion. To the extent that legal institutions embody these most basic informal institutions in the actual practices of a particular people, these institutions are beyond rational rejection. The electoral and law-making processes of a given people may faithfully reflect protocols for rational deliberation. These institutions would be immune to rational rejection wherever conditions made truth-seeking possible. But no one has ever claimed that the Constitution's decisional processes are congruent with practical reason itself.

Regarding constitutional rights, I repeat three earlier points: sane actors wouldn't leave a state of nature to protect themselves from government; rights don't protect rights, only power protects rights; and some rights can be integral to constitutional ends or to their pursuit. Free speech and fair trials can exemplify the latter, as long as the general population relies on them in good-faith pursuit of moral and nonmoral truth. For then they would be elements of truth-seeking processes that no one could in reason reject. Though free speech as truth-seeking and free speech as self-expression are radically different things, the latter may sometimes function as an element of the former. Madison's theory of interest representation serves as an example. The process of expressing private interests through elected representatives could have "[t]he effect of . . . refin[ing] and enlarge[ing] the public views, by passing them through the medium of a chosen body of citizens, whose wisdom may best discern the true interest of their country" (10:62). The adversarial trial might serve as another example. Though plaintiffs and defendants might have motives other than the truth, the court's aim should be the truth, and both sides giving their views of the facts under the rules of evidence improves the court's chances of arriving at the truth. A common feature of these examples is the presence of functionaries (legislators, judges) who are presumed to want the right thing.

The broadest claim of rights-oriented thinkers is that constitutionalism entails "a presumption of liberty," which amounts to a presumption in liberty's behalf against government's pursuit of its ends.[12] This "presumption of liberty" is altogether untenable. In practice it would mean that private individuals could do whatever they might want to do, just because they wanted to do it, and that government would have to show how restraining private actors would serve everyone's true interest, including the true interests of the persons whose conduct the government regulates. This "presumption of liberty" supposes a time in which private actors were and maybe still are free from any responsibility to others. They could do as they pleased as long as not prevented by laws to which they or their representatives had somehow freely chosen to submit. This presumption of liberty exists only in the musings of writers who ignore their own presuppositions; it can't describe human society of any kind, real or imagined. The presumption is defeated by language alone, the defining capacity of human kind.

Those of us who speak to each other do and must presuppose the rules of successful communication, like the rules of grammar and the moral rule that one should mean what one says. True, we don't always mean what we say. But even when we lie we rely on a moral rule against lying; we hope that others will follow that rule and assume that we also follow it. Lying would be futile if everyone always expected everyone else to lie or to tell the truth only when it served the speaker's calculated advantage. In fact communication of any sort would be impossible, actually inconceivable, if everyone always expected everyone else to lie or speak only on self-serving calculation. The same applies to the contracts that some thinkers imagine in a state of nature. People who contract with each other don't act in a normative vacuum. They could hardly contract with each other in a state of nature without language and the linguistic and moral rules attending communication in general (e.g., "mean what you say"), together with the moral and technical rules that constitute the practice of contracting (e.g., "keep your promises" and "do this for me, and I'll do that for you"). All of these most basic linguistic, technical, and moral rules get in the way of people's wants from time to time. Yet none of these rules could have been the conscious conclusion of an argument in the public interest, for if they didn't exist and govern human conduct with sufficient regularity, we would have no concept of a public, an argument, or an argument in the public interest.

We can observe the fallacy of this "presumption of liberty" by examining one of its best-known instances in American law, Justice Rufus Peckham's opinion for the Supreme Court in *Lochner v. New York* (1905).[13] In *Lochner* the Court held that the state of New York had no honest reason in the public interest to prescribe by law the maximum number of hours for work in bakeries. The liberty of labor and management to contract on mutually agreeable terms was the rule, with state regulation of contract terms the exception. The Court recognized exceptions in behalf of the health and safety of workers, and the state defended its law in these terms. But Justice Peckham and six of his brethren called the state's argument a pretext and held for the bakery. The bakery was not required to justify its demand that bakers work more than a sixty-hour week. And because only the state was required to give a reason for its regulation, this case and its many kindred cases across the fields of economic and morals legislation support the notion that private individuals can do whatever they want, without explaining or justifying themselves to the community, while the state can restrain private behavior only with a good reason. No such rule exists or can exist. We have already seen that communicative norms (restraints on private behavior) would be inconceivable if an actor of some kind (like "the community") had to justify the linguistic and moral rules governing communication. Certainly no such rule could exist in constitutional discourse, for if it did exist, following it would lead to contradiction.

Assume that the state can act only for good reasons while private individuals have a right to act for no reason at all unless prohibited by a rule enacted for what they could accept as a good reason. Imagine next that the state wants to act in a way that displaces an individual's private choice. To count as an act the state would need a reason or be imputed to have a reason, for a happening with no discernible or imputed reason would be an event in nature, not an act. If the individual had a right to act for any reason or none at all, no reason could defeat the best of reasons. That is, the individual could act from no reason to stop the state from acting for the best of reasons; the state could act only if the individual agreed, with no need whatever to justify his decision to anyone but himself. Now assume that the state decided to do something that some individual preferred not to do and the individual declared a right of private choice in the matter. The state would then have to forbear the good involved, which act of forbearance would be for no recognizable good at all. The state, in other words, would be obligated to honor the individual's arbitrary choice. This would make the state's action an arbitrary act, for there can be no reason to honor an arbitrary choice, and reason can't comprehend a rule favoring arbitrary choices over reasonable ones. But, *ex hypothesi*, the state can act only for a reason. The state that can act only for a reason could honor arbitrary private choices only if it could act for no reason, which would be absurd. Certainly, no such theory could comprehend a document that establishes coercive government and allows that decisions of this government are supreme law.

To avoid these difficulties we must distinguish a *restricted*, *restrained*, or *legitimate* sphere of privacy from an unjustified sphere of privacy. And, in fact, negative libertarians routinely make such a distinction, often in terms of *liberty* versus *license*.[14] The state is obliged to give a good reason only when it encroaches on *justified* privacy. But since what is justified is justified to someone, what is justified is publicly justified. The community alone decides what is justifiably private, therefore; the individual alone can't decide this question. No one starts with a presumption of privacy or liberty. We start with a presumption of *justified* liberty and all that this idea presupposes, including the practice of justifying claims and the complex idea of a well-ordered society that this practice would characterize. We can see these presuppositions at work in *Lochner*.

The situation in *Lochner* was not one in which an undefended private choice was entitled to an advantage that the public authority had to overcome with an argument. The situation was one in which two arguments competed with each other. Though Justice Peckham seemed to act on the maxim that liberty was the rule and regulation the exception, he was actually affirming a background argument that dominated his era and that favored the bakery. Two sub-arguments comprised this background argument for the bakery. One, a moral argument, claimed that in contract negotiations bargaining leverage lawfully obtained is property, and a just state takes property only when it has reason to believe doing so will benefit all sides. The other argument for the bakery was essentially a scientific argument. It claimed that security for lawfully obtained property (including bargaining power) enhances the prosperity of everyone. New York's argument is hard to describe because the argument that the state gave in court was probably a pretext, as Justice Peckham declared. Instead of saying that experience had disproved the contention about the universal benefits of an unregulated labor market, New York claimed that more than sixty hours a week in a bakery was unhealthy. But my point doesn't turn on the state's true reason. My point is that *Lochner* didn't vindicate liberty over government; *Lochner* chose between two different versions of the common good, each with its own view of the world, the ends of government, and justified liberties.

The Test of Constitutional Success

Only the positive view of the Constitution makes sense of constitutional language and history. Only a positive view of the Constitution fits a commonsense view of law and the world. Only a positive view of the Constitution avoids practical or logical absurdities. The test of constitutional success must therefore include a positive or ends-oriented test. Such a test would involve reasonable progress toward reasonable understandings of constitutional ends, good things like security, prosperity, and fairness. A constitution would be like a doctor's prescription. People wouldn't establish a government or change from one to the next unless there was something wrong with their present situation and they hoped government or a new government would make things better. If things got worse the government would be a bad government for them, and the constitution of a bad government would be a failed constitution.

A successful constitution would be one whose people and whose government made reasonable progress toward constitutional ends. And if such progress were the sole test we could move on to our remaining problems: a specification of constitutional ends and a test of progress toward them.

But the American Constitution envisions more than reasonable progress towards constitutional ends. We can see this by further reflection on what those ends might be. We now turn to that task.

3

Failure at What, Specifically?

The test of constitutional success or failure is reasonable progress toward, or irreversible fall from, the ends of government, as listed in the Constitution's preamble. I call this a "preambular test." Applying this test requires answering two questions: What ends does the Constitution envision? How do we know whether the nation is progressing toward or falling from these ends? Before turning to these questions, we should discuss several complications.

One Comprehensive End: The Good and Just Society

Constitution makers assume that the public purposes they seek are real goods attractive to all of the community's responsible members and that these different goods can be enjoyed together under the right circumstances. Yet, considered separately, the ends of the preamble may sometimes conflict. We can see this in the case of the common defense and domestic tranquility. Defending the nation may require material and psychological preparation for war, and such effort is hardly conducive to domestic tranquility. Consider also liberty. Though liberty's blessings is a preambular end, liberty may bring or maintain racial or class divisions that deny equal opportunity and therewith justice (retributive and distributive), another preambular end. The problem indicated here is not that preambular ends conflict with each other as do antithetical ideas, like freedom–slavery and justice–injustice. The problem is that people have conflicting conceptions of preambular ends and that even if they shared conceptions of different ends they could rarely enjoy at the same time all of the goods that the preamble lists. A government charged with pursuing multiple ends must therefore work to bring about or maintain social conditions of two kinds: conditions in which (1) the general public views the principal competing conceptions as good-faith understandings of one and the same general idea; and (2) the public believes that conditions in the country represent reasonable visions, under the circumstances, of all preambular ends taken together.

The assumption that constitutional ends are compatible in principle justifies embracing constitutional ends by some comprehensive good. *The Federalist* assumes such a comprehensive good throughout. In *Federalist* 40 Madison refers most often to the public's "happiness." In that same essay he also refers to "the public good" and "the real welfare of the great body of the people" (40:309). In a famous passage of *Federalist* 51 he says "justice is the end of government" and that it will be "pursued, until it be obtained, or until liberty be lost in the pursuit" (51:352). We shall see that it makes no practical difference which of these or equivalent terms we use as long as we assume that under ideal conditions preambular ends are mutually compatible and thus subsumable by a comprehensive idea and approachable through one set coordinated of means. Following Madison's example, I'll refer variously to the general welfare, the public happiness, the public good, and the like. I'll collect these terms under the more general idea of the Good and Just Society, and I'll discuss the "Large Commercial Republic," which summarizes Martin Diamond's theory of the Constitution's conception of the Good and Just Society.

A Mixed Logic

Our second complication involves constitutional logic. The Constitution has a mixed logical character, and this mixed character influences formulations of constitutional ends. The Constitution's basic normative property is that of means to ends. But constitutional interpretation can't be governed simply by an instrumentalist logic because the Constitution is also supreme law. The Constitution is not just means and not just law, but means and law together. And means-as-law makes sense only when the government and society under the law (the law in practice) is making reasonable progress toward the goods it was established to pursue, such as national defense and a general prosperity. An instrumental constitution makes sense to a particular population only when its members generally believe that the government and the society under the constitution is maintaining or making reasonable progress toward a good and just state of affairs.

Implications for Constitutional Change

What happens, then, when the system works not to pursue its ends but to defeat them? Jefferson's answer in the Declaration of Independence is: put up with abuses of government until they become unbearable and then revolt. Madison gives a more complicated answer in *Federalist* 40 but reaches essentially the same result: revolt when failure becomes unbearable. When Jefferson says that men change governments when abuses become unbearable, he eschews change for mere "light and transient causes." And before he declares independence he gives reasons that he assumes "a candid world" can understand—reasons understandable by all rational and mortal beings who live by exchanging reasons with one another about what to believe and what to do.

Madison takes a different path to revolutionary change. He says that as a principle of law and "plain reason," if the parts of a legal command can't be reconciled through interpretation, the less important should give way to the more important—"the means should be sacrificed to the end, rather than the end to the means" (40:260). Madison holds that this approach represents a deeper fidelity to the law because the law's sole aim is "the happiness of the people" (ibid.). We have seen him insist upon this course in *Federalist* 40, where he justifies bypassing Article XIII of the Articles of Confederation. Madison's result is similar to Jefferson's because bypassing Article XIII was a revolutionary act. It changed an existing constitution in a manner not allowed by that constitution, and the change was a big one; Hamilton called it "an alteration in the first principles and main pillars of the [existing] fabric" (15:93).

I emphasize, however, that neither Jefferson nor Madison treated the law of their day, flawed as it was, as mere means. Both submitted extensive arguments for disregarding the old law, and both invoked the only consideration that can account for the original decision to establish coercive authority: the need for government as means to common goods like security and prosperity, means to better things for all. Jefferson and Madison assumed an obligation to justify treating particular laws as means when the laws-as-means had failed, that is, when they had failed the ends for which they had been established. This assumed obligation to justify unauthorized change for the sake of the ends of law combined the law's obligatory and instrumental logics. This combination subordinated the legal to the instrumental, however, because the laws in question were of human origin and assumed the rationality and moral equality of all who were subject to the laws.

Aspirations and Obligations, Together

Ends like justice, security, and the general welfare are ends that people pursue, not necessarily realize. These ends are approachable; they don't have to be, and in fact can't be, fully and finally achievable. They are best understood as aspirations, like health. Mortals can never achieve healthy bodies, for as mortals they bear a potential for death, and in that respect they can never be simply healthy. The same applies to preambular ends: prosperity on earth always comes with potential collapse, justice on earth with potential relapse. Ethical theorists have thus found that aspirations are not subject to the principle of practical reason that "ought implies can." Unachievable ends—the objects of "aspirations" strictly speaking— are therefore not fairly mandated by law. Law, in reason, can only mandate conduct that is within the capacities (material, psychological, etc.) of most people. So whatever the ends of government might be, the Constitution could expect no more of its subjects than doing their best to pursue those ends in their lives and the lives of their countrymen, present and future. The same applies to observers of a nation's performance. "Failure" connotes blame that renders it less than fully appropriate for a country that's doing its best, even if its efforts are for naught.

Looking Ahead to a Problem with No Remedy

Aspirations are objects of desire; no law compelled the constituent authority ("We the People") to set forth its aspirations and establish a government to pursue them. The people did this because it wanted to, not because it had to. Laws, on the other hand, define duties, things we ought to do despite our wants. A constitution that combines aspirations and obligations assumes the coexistence of two attitudes among its subjects: a *desire* to follow the constitution, left over from the desire to establish it, and a sense of *duty* to follow it. We shall see in chapter 4, which takes up "the leader-follower problem," that constitutional success depends on whether the Constitution can evoke these attitudes in different kinds of people *and* whether these different kinds of people actually work together in progressive pursuit of the common good. This pursuit will often feature disagreement about whether the country is doing its best, for any such judgment will embody the limitations of fallible observers, and the Constitution's mixed logic supposes fallible actors. Ethical theorists have noticed that law presupposes an inclination to disobey; laws might compel kids to eat broccoli, but not ice cream. Fidelity to the Constitution as law would therefore entail (1) an awareness of this inclination and (2) a self-critical attitude, a habit of questioning our immediate wants and our unreflective conceptions of what's good. Should the community's opinion leaders be faithful to the law, the subject of public debate at any given moment would be not what the public wanted or believed. It would be what the public ought to want and could, with the right leadership, pursue. All would recognize, as both Hamilton and Madison did, that in a regime that is both democratic and constitutional, the highest task of political leadership is to educate the public from its initial inclinations to what good faith and full deliberation indicate about the public's true interests (63:424–425; 71:482–483).

At this writing, for example, the American public may want cheap gas more than energy independence. Many of us would contend that the public ought to want energy independence, and that the public therefore ought to appreciate the need for higher fuel taxes. We would engage people on the other side of this issue who claim that they too want energy independence but that higher taxes are not the way to achieve it. They claim that domestic energy reserves together with expected technological advance are sufficient for energy independence now and in the future, and that the solution is "drill, baby, drill" and tax subsidies that encourage both drilling and technological innovation. Because neither of the public positions on this issue openly denies an obligation to future generations, and because questions like the projected rate of oil consumption, likely quantity of reserves, and probable rate of technological advance are resolvable in principle, constitutionalists could expect both sides to debate in good faith and follow where the evidence leads.

Since "evidence" in this context means evidence of what is truly in the public interest, constitutionalists have little to say either to persons who aren't really interested in this kind of evidence *or* to persons who deny its existence. This includes ideologues whose chief interest is not truth but their conception of truth (a form of self-assertion), and academic value-skeptics who deny that real evidence can settle all the relevant questions. I mean to suggest by this example that, at present, two cultures share some responsibility for impending constitutional failure in America. One culture is comprised of religious and free-market zealots who know to a moral certainty that reality is as they see it; the other culture, comprised of moral skeptics mostly in the social sciences and academic law, denies that reality has any bearing on the value disagreements at the bottom of political disputes. The Scylla of dogmatism and Charybdis of skepticism have stalled and threatened to sink the American experiment in self-government.

Now to the question of constitutional ends.

The Large Commercial Republic

Disagreement about ends is the problem that vexes an ends-oriented constitutionalism and its preambular test of constitutional success and failure. Disagreement about ends explains the initial attractiveness of a process theory of constitutional success and failure. Americans generally agree on what offices the Constitution establishes, the basic functions of these offices, and the lawful occupants of these offices.[1] Not that structural issues are missing from constitutional debate in America—witness the debates between states' rights federalism and national federalism, majoritarian democracy and constitutional democracy, and positive and negative theories of the separation of power.[2] It's the nature of these issues. Closely examined, they involve not the identity of offices and officers but the nature and extent of their powers. Americans have no questions about who sits on the Supreme Court, for example, or what the Court's basic functions are; they divide on questions of the nature and extent of judicial power—whether, when, and on what grounds the Court should void decisions of coordinate branches. Americans also agree that the Constitution envisions two levels of government, national and state; they disagree about the principles for resolving conflicts among these levels of government. Viewing structural issues as questions not so much of structures but of the powers and rights of different institutions vis-à-vis each other, we can say that Americans generally agree on the most basic structural questions involving constitutional offices, officers, and functions. As for the logical difficulties of road-to-nowhere proceduralism, we have seen that the only coherent form of process constitutionalism is a form of positive constitutionalism that confounds public purposes with the expression, aggregation, and satisfaction of private ends.[3] The question, then, is whether a coherent (road-to-somewhere) proceduralism or structuralism can support a plausible theory of constitutional ends.

Diamond's Commercial Republic

The Federalist has been the most authoritative interpretation of constitutional structures over the centuries, and the most widely influential interpretation of *The Federalist* over the last two generations is the one Martin Diamond formulated in the 1950s. Though Diamond has his critics, no one denies that his is one of the historically reasonable interpretations of what leading framers (Hamilton especially) envisioned in the late 1780s. The attraction of Diamond's account is its ends orientation, its citizen's perspective on the Founding, and its focus on founding principles that are sufficiently general to accommodate changed conceptions. Diamond thus treated equal economic opportunity as a constitutional aspiration despite the founding generation's failure to live by that principle. Such attribution to the framers is controversial, but not unique.

Lincoln, Frederick Douglass, and others made similar claims when they said slavery offended founding principles and that the Constitution put slavery "in the course of ultimate extinction." Even if we could move beyond historical plausibility to historical certitude, plausibility suffices here, for no politically significant attribution to "the framers" is beyond challenge, and, I submit, the correct theory of constitutional failure assumes some disagreement about the right conception of ends.

Diamond focused more on the arguments in play at the Founding than on the personal histories, economic interests, and political relationships among the founding's leading figures. His remarkable discovery was the essentially Hamiltonian character of the original argument for ratifying the Constitution. Diamond showed that despite Madison's later split with Hamilton, Hamilton and Madison shared more or less the same vision of the nation's future during the ratification campaign, and it was what would later be known as a Hamiltonian vision. Diamond showed, in other words, that the American founding was a Hamiltonian moment. Diamond discovered this through an extensive analysis of *The Federalist* that centered on Madison's signature contribution to Western thought, the large-republic argument of *Federalist* 10. It argues, in the main, that majorities that sacrifice the public interest to their unreflective preferences will eventually kill popular government; that the solution to this problem is a large republic whose many interest groups will force government by shifting coalitions; and that the discipline of coalition building will weaken the prospect of stable coalitions for unjust purposes.

Diamond noticed that Madison's scheme depends on background economic and social-psychological conditions. A republic with a large territory and a large population doesn't guarantee a

politics of shifting majority coalitions open to all political interests as potential coalition partners. A large population occupying
a large territory could still be polarized along several axes, such as
religion, class, and political ideology. What Madison's theory needs
is a large number of interest groups that are willing to bargain with
each other. And whether there is a large number of the right kind
of groups depends on the values of the people who make up those
groups, specifically, whether they strive most for the kinds of goods
that can be compromised. Goods associated with religious zeal and
ideological zeal don't fit this description; wealth does. Madison
therefore presupposed a materialistic people, interested more in
things like security and plenty than obeying whatever God might
command or the glory of heroic risk and sacrifice for transcendent
causes. "[T]he most common and durable source of factions, has
been the various and unequal distribution of property," not a "zeal
for different opinions concerning religion, concerning Government and many other points," says *Federalist* 10 (10:58–59).

Notwithstanding his later alliance with Jefferson, the author
of *Federalist* 10, or at least his argument, also presupposed an urban-industrial society, for an agrarian society wouldn't have the
large number of economic interest groups necessary for the politics of shifting coalitions that *Federalist* 10 envisions. This urban-
industrial society would be committed also to the economic growth
and upward mobility needed to keep people focused on economic
ends as opposed to such uncompromisable ends as religious purity.
Equal opportunity and upward mobility for persons of merit would
be necessary to prevent political polarization along class lines. Notwithstanding slavery at the time of the Founding, *Federalist* 10 presupposes a people committed to equal opportunity and to a significant extent salutary results, for, said Diamond, "it is especially

the lowly, from whom so much is to be feared, who must feel least barred from opportunity and most sanguine about their chances . . . fragmented interests must achieve real gains from time to time, else the scheme ceases to beguile and mollify."[4]

Diamond thus concluded that *Federalist* 10 presupposes an urban-industrial society committed to economic growth, equal opportunity, and upward mobility for responsibly productive persons. In a later work Diamond proposed that the workings of this society would foster such distinctive personal virtues as the desire for wealth through socially responsible production. Diamond called this desire "acquisitiveness" and distinguished it from "greed," which he defined as the desire solely to possess wealth. Acquisitiveness also required discipline and moderation of the passions as needed to acquire skills for work that others will pay for. Honesty and promise-keeping were also virtues prized in a way of life centered on contract and commercial intercourse. "Finally," said Diamond in carefully chosen words and, he added, "with a brevity disproportionate to importance, one should also note gratefully, that the American political order, with its fluctuating and heterogeneous majorities and with its principle of liberty, supplies a not inhospitable home to the love of learning . . . [which occupies] a respectable distance indeed from its foundation in . . . [the] policy of opposite and rival interests," Madison's solution to the problem of majority faction.[5] This, then, is Diamond's Large Commercial Republic: a commercial yet democratic society that fosters acquisitiveness, secures equal opportunity for the poor, and provides a "not inhospitable home to the love of learning."

Diamond's observation about a home for the love of learning was far from a throwaway line. If, as he said, the importance of this observation is disproportionate to its brevity, then it is his most important observation. Others may adhere to the American Constitution and its way of life for their own reasons, mostly the love of gain; Diamond's personal reason was the place Americans provided for the love of learning.[6] Our question is what might the connection be between the Large Commercial Republic and the love of learning? What might Diamond have meant by the suggestion that the latter had its foundation in the former yet occupied a respectable distance from it? By the example of his career Diamond indicated that this "respectable distance" was a place from which an intellectual like him could respect the Large Commercial Republic even though its values were different from his own.[7] If we assume that Diamond respected the regime as he described it, his respect depended not only on the nation's hospitality to well-meaning criticism by people like himself, but on maintaining equality of opportunity, real gains for the poor, and a meaningful distinction between "acquisitiveness" and "greed." Diamond indicated further that his motivation for defending the American way was his own desire to be a certain kind of person, his desire to repay the Large Commercial Republic a benefit (providing him a place) for which he pointedly expressed his gratitude.

Though the acquisitive denizens of the Large Commercial Republic may not appreciate it, they owe a mutual debt to the likes of Diamond. Recall in this connection a matter discussed in chapter 2: the inability of the self-serving to defend self-service as a regime. Self-service as a regime is a public good and, as such, can't be appreciated by the self-serving themselves. Americans should infer as much from their own experience with slavery. Did not many of America's self-serving once practice slavery, denying that others had a right to serve themselves? Diamond, a lover of learning not wealth, could see reasons in the common good for defending a love of wealth. Yet Diamond knew that what justifies a practice limits it, and his reasons for supporting the acquisitive regime would have moderated the pursuit of wealth as needed to secure aspects of social justice relating to the opportunities and well-being of the poor. Diamond would have ennobled (in a sense socialized) the love of wealth by reconceiving it as a desire for wealth-getting through productive service to others. Diamond was thus able to defend the Large Commercial Republic in a way that its self-serving denizens could not, for the self-serving as such lack the magnanimity it takes to frame institutions that serve public purposes or to project themselves into that role. The self-serving thus have reason to be grateful to Diamond; he tried to make them look good. But can the self-serving appreciate this debt? Could they possibly put into practice the relationship between science and business represented in Diamond's writings? Would the self-serving be self-serving if they could appreciate this debt? I'll argue in due course that the success of the American regime probably depends on an affirmative answer to this question, and that the answer is probably no. (I say probably no because no one can rule out miracles.) But first I must comment on the relationship between the acquisitive life and the life of learning and connect that relationship to the ends of government and the preambular test for constitutional failure and success.

Beyond the Large Commercial Republic: A Healthy Politics

I remind the reader of my principal contentions so far:

- The Constitution is written as if its preambular goods are both real goods and social states of affairs, not merely governmental states of affairs. These real social goods are subsumable under one comprehensive term, like the Good and Just Society. But this society attracts competing conceptions. Because no one desires what he thinks are merely apparent goods, and because the Constitution's legal aspect assumes an inclination to disobey, fidelity to the Constitution demands a self-critical attitude toward one's initial conceptions of the Good and Just Society and a willingness to adopt better conceptions as the evidence indicates.

- The evidence in question is not privileged evidence; it is available to all on the basis of firsthand human experiences, in principle to the "candid world" addressed by the Declaration of Independence. The universally shareable evidence that supports successful conceptions of the Good and Just Society rules out sectarian conceptions of that society supported by hearsay (such as scripture) and communicated through clerical authority. The secular nature of the Good and Just Society is indicated also by the Constitution's prohibition of religious tests for office, which, in a democracy where citizens are eligible for office, implies no religious test for citizenship. No religious test for the rights to make, administer, and review the community's decisions regarding life and death, ways and means.

- A preambular test of constitutional success and failure is more persuasive than its rivals because the preambular test is the only one consonant with the constitutional text, the history of the American founding, the principles of practical reason, and the need to make sense of obedience to law.

- The most influential of the ends-oriented constitutionalists is Martin Diamond. Though Diamond saw the Constitution as dedicated to the Large Commercial Republic, he defended that regime from a perspective that valued intellectual pursuits more than wealth, and he shaped his vision of the Large Commercial Republic accordingly. Specifically, Diamond defended the Large Commercial Republic only insofar as it supported science for the sake of science (Diamond's "love of learning") and moderated the pursuit of wealth as needed for equal opportunity and realistic hope of upward mobility for all, especially the poor.

Aristocracy within Mass Democracy

Diamond's Large Commercial Republic is a republic of the acquisitive, not the greedy, for as between greed and acquisitiveness, only the latter can be justified. This follows from the nature of justification. Justifying something is a discursive act that most immediately involves two people, a speaker and an auditor, against the background of a functioning society. The occasion for this act is the transformation of a mere spectator of another's conduct (opinion, attitude, etc.) into an auditor of the other's conduct. This transformation occurs when the spectator sees something in the conduct of another not only of which he may disapprove but of which the larger community may disapprove. When the spectator sees something questionable in the conduct of another, he may ask for a justification, and when he does, he assumes the stance of one who represents the community. Justification occurs when the original actor successfully shows that conduct that initially seemed harmful to others (and thus called for justification) actually benefited others, for like any actor, the community (and anyone who represents it) values only what it thinks is good for itself. Justifying something therefore presupposes a common good, actors who can serve the common good, and auditors who are devoted to the common good. "Acquisitiveness" was Diamond's name for self-service that also served the common good. It was his way of distinguishing self-service that could be justified from self-service that could not be justified.

Diamond was led to his saving rendition of American acquisitiveness by his Socratic understanding of human nature. Human beings, he reasoned, were distinguished from other beings by their capacity to transcend their animal nature and associated pleasures and direct their conduct toward what reason disclosed as truly good, not just apparently good. Because reason presupposes a society, the good that reason discloses can't be antisocial. This rules out purely self-serving conduct with no net social benefit. On occasions when self-serving conduct appears harmful to others, it cannot be defended to others if it remains purely self-serving. Diamond condemned purely self-serving conduct and distinguished a socially beneficial form of self-serving conduct. By this interpretive act of shaping the distinguishing American characteristic (acquisitiveness) into a virtue (socialized acquisitiveness), Diamond led from behind, so to speak: he implicitly elevated what he called "mind" and "the love of learning" to a position of power over wealth, which was the Socratic view of the only viable relationship among human goods and corresponding authorities.

Seeking to secure wisdom's influence to the extent that he could under modern circumstances, Diamond urged American higher education to immerse its students in the literature of the American founding, which he considered wisdom's moment in America. Yet Diamond sought more than to perpetuate the conclusions of the founders. Though he did feel that all but the very brightest students should be taught to venerate those conclusions, he sought most to cultivate students who could take issue with the Founding in the respectful and constructive manner exemplified by his own career. Diamond accepted Leo Strauss's definition of liberal education as "the ladder by which we try to ascend from mass democracy to democracy as originally meant," which amounts to "the necessary endeavor to found an aristocracy within democratic mass society."[8] Strauss's comment neatly describes Diamond's rendition of the Founding. It also shows that Diamond discerned a constitutional end higher than a large commercial republic, namely, a large commercial republic whose conception of wealth and justice was shaped by people who valued truth above wealth.

The Constitution of a Healthy Politics

Indeed, the Large Commercial Republic cannot be the Constitution's ultimate end. That result is precluded as a matter of semantics and constitutional logic. As a sheer matter of English usage, "Good and Just Society" isn't synonymous with "Large Commercial Republic." As Diamond conceived the Large Commercial Republic, its features may be necessary if the system outlined in *Federalist* 10 is to work as Madison planned, and these features can serve as conceptions of preambular ends and therewith the Good and Just Society. But conceptions of a general idea may be mistaken as a matter of theory and made false in practice by circumstances. Diamond's Large Commercial Republic can hardly be the Good and Just Society if it is not viable in practice. And it can't exist for long if there's no way to prevent its degeneration into an oligarchy where great wealth uses its power over the universities and the mass media to degrade political philosophy to ideology and persuade the public that freedom and prosperity entail the power to bribe politicians, strangle opportunities for the poor (on the canard that poverty is usually deserved), and reduce labor, which actually produces goods and services, to supplication.

Were Diamond's regime actual and stable, it would still be but a conception of the Good and Just Society. Well-being as wealth and the competence to acquire it did not constitute Diamond's personal understanding of well-being, and it's not beyond contention that they work for others. Bourgeois modernity is attractive to all reflective people when compared to life under the "spiritual" powers of sixteenth- and seventeenth-century Europe. But things have moved on to overpopulation, diminishing natural resources, and greenhouse. And even if these threats to modernity were exaggerated, recent research suggests that people in the market democracies would be happier with less economic mobility and more stable families, friendships, and communities.[9] Assume the Constitution is what it says it is, an instrument of things like the peoples' welfare, and acknowledge the gap between any conception of well-being and the real thing, and people who are really well off will appear to be not necessarily the denizens of the Large Commercial Republic but people who can do what the founding generation did: assess their problems and fashion institutions to meet them. A constitution adequate to real ends in a world of contingencies will preserve the capacity for constructive social and governmental change. Whether Americans still have this capacity is something we can surely doubt. I'll say more about this problem in chapter 5.

The Large Commercial Republic is mistakenly confounded with the Good and Just Society for yet another reason, this one having to do with Article V of the Constitution. As a conception of constitutional ends the Large Commercial Republic is dubious because of the widespread sense that the Constitution is "made for people of fundamentally differing views" and "is not intended to embody a particular economic theory," as Justice Oliver Wendell Holmes put it in a famous dissent.[10] Though one can disagree with Justice Holmes, as Diamond did and as I do, Holmes's point is defensible. Grant, contra Holmes, that protection for private property is expressly available under the Fifth and Thirteenth Amendments and implicit in the Fourth Amendment and Congress's power (and therewith duty) to secure the property rights of authors and inventors. Grant also that the Constitution's structures can work as originally planned only in the Large Commercial Republic. Grant further that a commercial life is compatible with the life of science and the autonomous intellect for a reason of central importance: they both see evidence of truth as experiential of this world and shareable by humanity at large. Grant all these things and the Large Commercial Republic would still be but a reasonable conception of preambular ends *under present institutional arrangements and world conditions.* But the world changes, and the rights, powers, and structures of the present institutional arrangement are all amendable. The amendability of present structures renders less than fundamental a conception of constitutional ends that is derived from those structures.

The amendability of constitutional provisions and the need to connect a theory of constitutional ends to the constitutional text might indicate that there can be no ultimate, final, or unchangeable constitutional end. But this is not the case, for one feature of the Constitution is not amendable, and this feature is amendability itself, a property that constitutes a normative principle, the principle of amendability. The current expression of this principle is the Constitution's Article V. Article V replaces Article XIII of the Articles of Confederation. In chapter 2 of this book I follow Madison in *Federalist* 40 and contend that the founding generation was right to ignore Article XIII because it had ceased to function as a path to needed amendments and was therefore no longer a meaningful amending rule. The principle of amendability should be distinguished from particular amending rules. Amending rules are tools crafted for particular communities to effect institutional change when needed. The principle of amendability holds that a rationally defensible constitution will contain an amending rule. If as a matter of either public opinion or objective moral fact the community needs constitutional change and change doesn't materialize, then its particular amending rule ceases to be what it purports to be and there can be no reason to honor it.

Madison went further. Beyond no reason to respect a failed amending rule, he recognized an affirmative duty to ignore a failed amending rule. He claimed that the Convention, the Congress that authorized the Convention, and the state legislatures that were calling ratifying conventions—that all these "servants of their country" had an affirmative duty to ignore Article XIII. For letting a small minority obstruct needed change would effectively deny "the transcendent and precious right of the people to 'abolish or alter their governments as to them shall seem most likely to effect their safety and happiness'" (40:265–267). To honor this right and serve what the framers saw as the nation's objective needs, they acted outside the law—outside the law's amending rule as required under the circumstances by the principle of amendability itself. This principle of amendability is the Constitution's implicit recognition of nature's primacy over social convention and reason's greater attraction to nature. An insistence on Article XIII would have elevated convention over nature and subordinated reason to convention, for nothing supported Article XIII beyond the historical fact of its establishment, which by itself is no reason at all, *and* the Antifederalist claim that adhering to prior establishments, even indefensible ones, was a necessary hedge against chaos. By rejecting this counsel, the delegates at Philadelphia, and eventually the country, acknowledged the primacy of reason and nature over normatively opaque social convention.

In a way, the Philadelphia Convention acted in the only way it could. Though it could have told Congress that it could make no proposal, in view of the conviction that change was needed, failure to make a proposal would have been failure to act due to unavailable means; it would not have been a proposal that no change was needed. Or the Convention might have proposed changes through Article XIII. But this act would have been pointless unless the delegates held some hope that pressure from cooperating states would be too much for the obstructionist minority—in which case they would have considered Article XIII more than a pointless formalism. Submitting proposed change to an admittedly hopeless process would have been a mysterious event, not a real act. The Convention's adherence to an admittedly empty formalism could not have been seen as an act because it would have departed from foundational truths of practical science: that all actors act for what they think is some good *and* with the expectation that their conduct just might cause the good to materialize. Those who insisted on Article XIII must therefore have seen it as an effective means to *some* good. And this is precisely how Madison understood some of the Convention's critics: their "ill-timed scruples" and "zeal for adhering to ordinary forms" were but "masks" for their "secret enmity" to the proposed national government (40:265). Insisting on Article XIII was simply a way to kill the proposed constitution. But the Philadelphia Convention was proposing this very constitution.

One could understand *the Convention's* adherence to an unworkable rule only by some further attribution, like the satisfaction that might attend an act of futile protest.

As an expression of reason's affinity to nature, the principle of amendability is itself unamendable. To amend this principle would be to abandon it, and people can't chose to live by subordinating reason to any authority whose decrees they can't connect ultimately to what ordinary men and women see as some good. This holds even for individuals who are far from ordinary. God promised Abraham leadership of an empire as reward for the otherwise pointless act of sacrificing Isaac. Socrates described the rewards of philosophy as pleasures even greater than the most intense pleasures of the body. And Jesus held out to believers the possibility of everlasting life. None of these prospects would have made sense without the value that ordinary people place on mundane things like dominion, pleasure, and life.

That one can't choose to live without thinking for one's self about what's good and evil follows from the nature of choice, reason, and action. Choosing something is an act, at least of the mind, and action is always for the sake of something that the actor thinks is good. The result of an act is (generally understood to be) a state of affairs that didn't have to materialize and wouldn't have materialized save for the intention of the actor, which could have been otherwise. The good for which the act is performed is the reason for the act. If an observer can see no consequence of a subject's movement that he thinks the subject would regard as both good and optional, then the observer can't impute action to the subject. The observer can allege causality, but not agency. He can say that the subject moved and that something happened as result, but not that the subject chose the result or acted to bring it about. Action without a reason is therefore not action, and since to choose is to act, one can't choose to live without the capacity to form independent judgments about ends and means. The same holds for communities that make constitutions. Their constitutions must include amending rules, for the effectiveness of rules depends on contingencies that change, rules that no longer work are pointless, to accept pointless authority is to choose to live without reason, and that's impossible. Though slavery of the body can befall a person or a community, slavery can be chosen as a way of life only by actors who see it as a way to avoid a greater calamity, like death. It can't be chosen as an end. Though one can choose a course, like suicide, that results in no further choice, one can't choose to live without the capacity to decide between good and evil, for without this capacity one can't act, and where one can perform no act at all, one can't choose.[11]

This unamendability of amendability brings us back to what *Federalist* 1 treats as the world-historical significance of the ratification campaign and the image that the founding generation sought to project to the world—that is, what the nation wanted to appear to others to be and therefore wanted actually to be. The passage is well known in which Hamilton says that mankind looks to America to prove man's capacity "to establish good government from reflection and choice" and to avoid government based "on accident and force" (1:3). Had Hamilton been right to treat the ambition to rational government as an ambition of man as man, it would be shared by all generations. From the perspective of later generations, the only reason to choose to live under constitutions and constitutional rules that no longer worked would be to avoid greater misfortunes. Where no such calculation occurred periodically and on a sufficiently broad scale, people would no longer choose their government by reflection and choice; they would simply live where a fortunate or an unfortunate fate had deposited them, with no power to change in either case. People can live such a life; in fact, virtually everyone does. But no one would choose either fate for the same reason that no one would choose to live a vegetative existence, however healthy.

A life worth choosing therefore depends on the scope of its possessor's capacity and opportunity for reflection and choice regarding both ends and means. Reflection is not following inclinations but examining them, and reflection is pointless if one is unwilling or unable to change course. Choice depends on the power to act as reflection indicates. The same holds for a political community. A community that lives by reflection and choice is one whose decision makers exchange reasons with each other about the community's proper direction and effective and affordable ways and means, and one that actually changes for the better from time to time. If the community is a democracy, where consent is a necessary condition for legitimacy, change will tend to be for the better and perceived by all responsible factions as either for the better or a good-faith and reasonable move for the better. A sense of fallibility and mutual good faith is a crucial element of this situation. Hamilton thus reminds readers of *Federalist* 1 that "we upon many occasions, see wise and good men on the wrong as well as on the right side of questions, of the first magnitude to society," and that reflection on this fact "would furnish a lesson of moderation to those who are ever so much persuaded of their being in the right, in any controversy" (1:4–5). The politics of a community whose members followed this advice would be a healthy politics. And where preambular ends are seen as real goods that invite competing conceptions, the end of government can only be the pursuit of the ends of government through a healthy politics. I grant that this is a visionary aim, but it is not utopian in the sense of other-worldly. Nor is it more visionary than its objects, like real and lasting national security and prosperity.

What, then, are the ends of government? How do we know we're progressing toward them? One phrase answers both questions: a healthy politics. A politics marked by reasonable and good-faith disagreement about ends thought to be real goods, goods about which people can be wrong, and therefore goods whose content and means are disclosed through an exchange of evidence that is based on common human experience, as opposed to privileged revelation.

4

Constitutional Failure: Mostly (Though Not Entirely) Attitudinal

Our discussion to this point indicates that constitutional failure is mostly a matter of public and elite attitudes. A preambular test of constitutional failure and success is the true test because only a theory of the Constitution as an instrument of its ends can describe ratifying the Constitution as a rational act and make sense of the Constitution's claim on people's continuing allegiance. Because the Constitution's basic normative property is means-as-law, the Constitution assumes either that two kinds of people are coexisting in one national community or that the typical American is a person in whom two attitudes coexist. One attitude or kind of person values the Constitution mostly as means to desirable public goods; the other accepts the Constitution mostly as binding law. The former, as a type of person, wants to be and to be seen by others as a benefactor or as part of a project that benefits others. Persons of this type are like those that the American founders and other statesmen claimed to be: like Washington they want to found great nations or, like Lincoln and Roosevelt, they want to preserve great nations. Hamilton assumed that Americans of the 1780s had some of this great-souled character in them when he appealed in *Federalist* 1 to their patriotic and philanthropic ambition to display mankind's capacity to establish good government from reflection and choice (1:3). Madison assumed the same in *Federalist* 14 when he praised the framers of the nation's state constitutions for preferring "their own good sense . . . and . . . experience" over traditional authorities. "Happily for Americans," he said, "happily we trust for the whole human race, they pursued a new and more noble course" than "blind veneration for antiquity, for custom, or for names" (14:88–89).

A different attitude or kind of person will accept the Constitution, if at all, less from aspiration than from a sense of obligation. People of this type understand their private pursuits as separated from public purposes. Though they may confine their self-service to lawful channels, they do so originally either from fear or from "enlightened self-interest," a concomitant of fear, and eventually from habit. Constitutional success or failure depends ultimately on a relationship between the attitudes of constitutional aspiration and constitutional obligation and their corresponding human types. Constitutional failure and success turn eventually on the degree of political influence enjoyed by people who see something universally admirable in the Constitution as a political project and who aspire to advance that project, a social state of affairs, the preceding chapter's "Good and Just Society." The constituent of this end (its "constitution") is a pairing of specific human types, a pairing of persons who actively aspire to demonstrate government by reflection and choice and persons who act from a sense of obligation to that government.

These results are corollaries of constitutional logic: The Constitution is means-as-law by its language, its history, and the principles of practical reason. Means-as-law is sensible and therefore obligatory only so long as it can reasonably be seen as an effective means to a desirable state of society. Because means are essentially contingent, a rational constitution would be, and in America's case is supposed to be, amendable. The Constitution's supposed amendability makes the Large Commercial Republic but a conception of, at best a step toward, some comprehensive good, like the public happiness that marks the Good and Just Society. Because a mere conception of the good is not the good, amendability makes the Constitution's ultimate end something that's unamendable—something that no one can in reason reject. In the case of an individual, this undeniable good is thinking for oneself: no one can actively choose to live without thinking for oneself about what's good. In a community's case, thinking for oneself about what's good is the practice of choosing public policy by exchanging reasons on the basis of experiences that all parts of the community share. The shareability of experience and the impossibility of choosing to live without thinking for oneself preclude unquestioned submission to divine authority (impossible in any case after the Fall). They also preclude public action on the basis of private or privileged revelations. Public reason is therefore *secular* public reason. Public reason as a social practice implies public reasonableness—a disposition to account for one's actions to others in ways that others can understand and live with. This disposition is a virtue, and a publicly reasonable citizenry is therefore one way to describe the end of constitutional government. In practice this means either a general population whose typical member can reaffirm the Constitution as means to what reason discloses as the Good and Just Society or a community that trusts a leadership stratum that is capable of such determinations as conditions change, which they inevitably do. The very logic of the Constitution and its founding indicates that at bottom the American constitution is a relationship of human types that meets the requirements of "government by reflection and choice." If my argument is correct, constitutional failure and success are largely matters of the attitudes of leaders and followers. Further evidence for this conclusion is to be found in those occasions when the Constitution ceases to be the means-as-law that it says it is.

Two Cases

The American founding and the Civil War are occasions of institutional breakdown followed by dramatic institutional change. The Founding involved the collapse of a confederation; the Civil War involved the collapse of a federation. The confederation failed to meet the needs of its people; the federation proved unable to maintain a united people. Yet *institutional* breakdown and *constitutional* breakdown may not be the same thing, and institutional breakdown notwithstanding, neither the Founding nor the Civil War may be a case of constitutional breakdown. Indeed, from Madison's account of the Founding, the Confederation might even appear as something of a success. After all, officials of the Confederation oversaw fundamental institutional reform through peaceful means, a feat the nation was not to repeat and probably won't repeat.[1] And as Lincoln saw it, the Civil War represented less a breakdown of the Constitution than the "rebirth" of its founding principle.

True, both the Founding and the Civil War marked cases of institutional failure and extralegal, even illegal, routes to institutional change. Madison and Lincoln claimed continuity between the old and the new, and they may well have done so to give the changes they sought a veneer of legality. On the other hand, we don't have to take the claims of Madison and Lincoln as window dressing, for if our reflections on constitution logic are sound, we can and should construe Madison and Lincoln as having claimed not institutional continuity but constitutional continuity, continuity of constitutional principle. History, after all, doesn't speak for itself. To have current significance past events must be seen as "cases" of some presently interesting pattern of events, and transforming an event into a case of practical significance requires the event's refraction through a moral medium. However we might view the Founding and the Civil War in other contexts, here they can reasonably be read to show that great institutional change need not be constitutional change and that constitutional change is essentially an attitudinal affair.

From the Articles to the Constitution

We've seen that the Constitution's amendability precludes any suggestion that fidelity to the Constitution is fidelity to the Constitution's precise language at any given moment, including its amending rule. Amendability implies fallibility and assumes that change can be good, even for a constitution. The Constitution's amending rule is no exception; it came from fallible minds, and it too can fail to be what it is supposed to be. Human beings would have to control the course of nature for them to fashion a method of amendment that worked in all circumstances, and an amending rule that doesn't work when and as it should, is not (really) an amending rule. We've also seen that fidelity to the Constitution is fidelity to background constitutional principles and that vindication of these principles

will inevitably require extralegal action. On this last point we recall Madison's observation that "all great changes of established
governments" originate in "*informal and unauthorized propositions*,
made by some respectable citizen or number of citizens," not by
officials acting according to law (40:265, his emphasis). From these
premises it would follow that under some conditions legally unauthorized institutional change need not mean constitutional change.
The conditions are (1) legal rules that have ceased to embody the
principles that justify their existence; (2) a movement that would
replace old rules with rules that do embody justifying principles; (3)
popular acceptance of the new rules. Thus, in appealing for popular
acceptance of the new Constitution through a procedure unauthorized by the old Article XIII, Madison claimed that the Articles of
Confederation as a whole, including Article XIII, had ceased to be
an instrument of the people's welfare and that the proposed constitution embodied the background principles of legitimacy that
both the Articles and popular government generally represented.

Regarding the new constitution's embodiment of old principles,
Madison gave several examples. In *Federalist* 45 he said that the
people's welfare was the supreme object of government and that no
form of government had any value save as means to this end. This
was the overarching principle of all American constitutions, said
Madison, and the proposed constitution expressed it better than
the Articles of Confederation. In *Federalist* 40 Madison descended
to institutional particulars. To those who felt that constitutional
principles included state legislative appointment of members of the
government, he said, the new constitution recognizes that principle
in its provision for a senate, whose members were originally elected
by the state legislatures. And to those who felt that constitutional
principles require "that the powers of the general government . . .

be limited," he said that the powers of the proposed government "are limited" and the states "in all unenumerated cases, are left in the enjoyment of their sovereign and independent jurisprudence." In sum, he added, "the great principles of the constitution proposed by the Convention, may be considered less as absolutely new, than as the expansion of principles which are found in the articles of Confederation" (40:261–262). These claims are a mixture of the compelling and the disingenuous. One can hardly disagree with Madison that the people's well-being is more important than the defeasible means to the people's well-being. Yet one can hardly accept this last tenet and then say that anything resembling a "fundamental principle" justifies either states' rights or the constitution of the U.S. Senate. Madison himself denied elsewhere in *The Federalist* and in private correspondence that there was anything "fundamental" about either states' rights or the Senate's composition.[2] Defensible or not, Madison's specific claims do not affect my point about the general maxim that his claims illustrate, namely, that when legal provisions no longer serve their justifying principles, the law, in reason, ceases to obligate, and fidelity to the principles calls for new measures, through extralegal means if need be.

Though Madison observed that great changes in the law came from unauthorized sources, Madison's situation was somewhat different. In his case, fidelity to higher principles was also a matter of legal obligation. This follows from the role Madison assumed as a spokesman for the Constitutional Convention, a body that Congress had charged with proposing constitutional changes that were "adequate to the exigencies of the Union." While the content of the Convention's proposals departed from existing law, the Convention itself was a lawfully created body charged with proposing changes to the law, and this body could reasonably claim, as Madison did, that its proposals embodied the law's deeper principles, especially the law's leading principle: that a constitution's sole value was as an instrument of the people's welfare. Moreover, when Madison helped formulate and later defend the Convention's proposals, he defended Congress as well as the Convention, for Congress had approved the Convention's proposals and sent them to the states for ratification. For these reasons, the Convention's plan was not altogether unauthorized, and Madison could claim not only a continuity of substantive principle between the Confederation and the Constitution, but also a continuity of procedure: Congress authorized the Convention; all but one of the states sent delegates; the Convention reported back to Congress; Congress submitted the proposals to the states; and no state was denied its right of consent. Such was Madison's attempt to claim consistency with established law.

Nevertheless, Madison conceded that the content of the Convention's plan departed from the law, especially the old amending rule, Article XIII. The new Article V was an unauthorized means to an authorized end, a government adequate to the nation's needs. This made the Convention's action mixed: in one respect it was lawful, in another respect it wasn't. As for the distinction between aspiration and obligation in Madison's case, again, the picture is mixed. Madison and his fellow framers acted inside the law in some respect and therefore coincidentally with their legal duty, but not chiefly from a sense of legal duty. Their legalistic defense of their conduct was but a minor part of their overall argument for ratification, which was plainly and unapologetically instrumental. One can therefore conclude that Madison and his allies acted outside the law and from a sense of aspiration, not legal obligation. The least one can say is that they acted more from aspiration than from obligation. The framers' attitude thus appears as a mixture of aspiration and obligation, with aspiration on top.

Lincoln's Case

By the time Lincoln addressed a special session of Congress on July 4, 1861, civil war had been underway for almost eleven weeks. Lincoln had placed a blockade on Southern ports; called 75,000 militiamen into federal service; added an additional 40,000 men to the Union's forces; purchased fifteen warships; committed $2 million to private contractors to recruit additional troops; suspended habeas corpus in sections of Maryland and Pennsylvania; instructed his generals to ignore an order of the chief justice of the United States; closed the U.S. mails to publications deemed disloyal to the union; and pledged the credit of the United States to pay for the military buildup—all without congressional authorization. Daniel Farber understates the matter by a mile when he says that Lincoln's "authority to do any of these things on his own was, to say the least, unclear." Farber says this because "[u]nder the Constitution, Congress rather than the president has the authority to declare war and to control the mails, the military, and the purse."[3]

Farber is generous to Lincoln. He carefully analyzes each of Lincoln's moves in light of both nineteenth-century and present-day legal standards and finds most of Lincoln's acts within arguable constitutional limits. Farber's reasons include early statutory authority (to call state militias into federal service and, arguably, blockade rebel ports);[4] congressional silence in emergencies and subsequent congressional approval of executive acts (regarding enlarging the Union's forces, unauthorized funding of early actions, and suspension of habeas);[5] and traditional doctrines of executive duty to protect public facilities and personnel and to respond to force initiated by others (authorizing return fire at Sumter and ordering federal troops into Maryland to ensure access to Washington).[6] Farber's chief reservations involve threats to civil liberties, specifically Lincoln's unauthorized suspension of habeas in the early days of the war, prior restraint of publications critical of the war, and military trial of civilians in areas of the North that lay beyond the threat of immediate hostilities.[7] Of special interest to us is the message Farber draws from Lincoln's argument for suspending habeas.

Within two weeks after Sumter's fall Maryland teetered toward rebellion, and pro-rebel mobs in Baltimore had obstructed union troop movements and severed rail connections to Washington. Lincoln responded by authorizing Winfield Scott, commanding general of the army, to suspend habeas "at any point on or in the vicinity of the military line which is now used between the city of Philadelphia via Perryville, Annapolis City and Annapolis Junction you find resistance which renders it necessary to suspend the writ of habeas corpus for the public safety." Lincoln authorized Scott to suspend the writ either "personally or through the officer in command at the point where resistance occurs." From his headquarters in Washington, Scott then delegated this authority to his generals in the field, and on April 27, 1861, Major General Robert Patterson suspended the writ in parts of Maryland. On May 25, Union troops arrested John Merryman, a prominent Baltimorean, for secessionist activities. On May 26, Roger Brooke Taney, chief justice of the United States, on circuit in Baltimore, issued a writ of habeas to General George Cadwalader, the commander of Ft. McHenry, where the army was holding Merryman without formal charge. In granting the writ, Taney reasoned that only Congress could suspend habeas since the power to do so was listed among the restraints on congressional power in Article I, Section 9, of the Constitution. Such was the understanding of authorities like John Marshall and Joseph Story, said Taney, and Congress's exclusive possession of this authority reflected Anglo-American traditions favoring legislative over executive power. Cadwalader refused to comply. Taney then ordered the general's arrest, but the sentries denied the marshal entry to the fort. Stating that no posse comitatus could overpower the fort, Taney exhorted Lincoln to enforce the court's authority, reminding him in the process of the president's duty to take care that the laws be faithfully executed. Lincoln ignored the lecture, and in his message to Congress of July 4, he stated why.[8]

Lincoln made two arguments, one from background principles that subordinate the positive law to the people's safety, the other partly (only partly) from textual premises. The argument from background principles came first. It set the tone and the frame of Lincoln's textual argument. Turning on rhetorical questions that shifted the moral burden from Lincoln to his congressional audience, the argument from principle ultimately altered the nature of Lincoln's textual argument. Lincoln started by claiming that he had suspended the writ in an emergency situation out of concern for "the public safety." He then addressed those who questioned the legality of his acts. Alluding to Taney, Lincoln said that "the country's attention has been called to the proposition that one who is sworn to 'take care that the laws be faithfully executed,' should not himself violate them." But the duty to "take care" applied to the "whole of the laws," he said, and "in nearly one-third of the States" the whole of the laws "were being resisted, and failing of execution." Must the whole of the laws be allowed to fail though it might be "perfectly clear" that the whole could be saved by violating a "single law, made in such extreme tenderness of the citizen's liberty, that practically, it relieves more of the guilty than of the innocent?" "[A]re all the laws *but one,* to go unexecuted, and the government itself go to pieces, lest that one be violated"?[9]

Though such was the question Lincoln posed to his audience, he began his legal argument by claiming that he could avoid this question because his suspension of the writ was, in fact, constitutional. The legal question was not whether *some* part of the government could suspend the writ if the public safety required it; Article I, Section 9, put that matter beyond dispute. The question was whether the *president* could suspend the writ—whether he could do so on his own, without congressional authorization. Citing text and traditional authority, Taney had claimed it to be "one of those points of constitutional law upon which there was no difference of opinion, and that it was admitted on all hands, that the privilege of the writ could not be suspended, except by act of congress."[10] But Lincoln exploited (fabricated?) a textual opening that enabled him to appeal to his audience's common sense. The textual opening lay in the phrasing of the writ suspension clause. Though the clause is located in Article I, the legislative article, and though it appears in a list of restraints that is expressly or by clear implication addressed to Congress alone, the clause itself does not say "*Congress* shall not suspend the writ, unless . . ."; it says that the writ "shall not be suspended, unless. . . ." This phrasing makes the clause the only member of its list that is not unquestionably addressed to Congress and Congress alone, and this allowed Lincoln to claim that "the Constitution is silent" as to who shall exercise the power. Then Lincoln invoked common sense. Since the clause "was plainly made for a dangerous emergency," he said, "it cannot be believed the framers of the instrument intended, that in every case, the danger should run its course, until Congress could be called together; the very assembling of which might be prevented, as was intended in this case, by the rebellion."[11]

Lincoln thus suggested an unanswerable point. Had the framers intended an exclusively congressional power, the power would have failed the reason for its existence: the need to meet rebellion or invasion, including unanticipated rebellion or invasion. This need favors an institution that, unlike a legislature and a court, is always in session, and can act with dispatch without a requirement of prior deliberation and approval by some collective body. It favors an institution that commands the armed forces, an institution that, unlike a court, can deal with illegality massed in the form of a general rebellion, as distinguished from the illegal acts of isolated individuals. By the nature of emergencies, therefore, power to suspend habeas in emergencies was properly an executive power, shareable with the legislative branch where feasible, perhaps, but still an executive power. Lincoln was to make this case explicit in two letters of June 1863.[12] Yet the framers had in fact listed the writ suspension clause in Article I, Section 9, and by so doing they appeared to have committed what Lincoln was effectively declaring a mistake—born, no doubt, of the old colonialist fear of executive power that had survived disappointments with legislative government under the Articles of Confederation. Lincoln's textual argument was therefore not simply a textual argument. It was rather an argument for a construction of the constitutional text that brought it closer to the demands of reality. Lincoln addressed this argument not to people willing to martyr the nation to the letter of the law—those perhaps like Taney, whose accumulated years made heaven's promises loom brighter than earth's rewards and who, for some reason, attached the letter of the law to heaven's promises. Lincoln addressed people who were in their right minds, people who wanted to win the war.

Farber (ever the lawyer?) would avoid a conclusion that Lincoln acted above the law in suspending habeas. Lincoln didn't claim immunity from the law, says Farber; he didn't claim "that pressing circumstances overrode the 'take care' duty to follow the law. He merely observed that he was faced with the utter impossibility of full compliance and had to choose the lesser of two evils."[13] I'd state the point somewhat differently because I don't regard choosing a necessary means to victory as an evil of any stripe merely because it goes against a constitutional provision that is devoid of moral import and that, if followed, would defeat its own purpose. I'd say that, like the Constitution as a whole, the writ suspension clause makes sense only in circumstances where it is a reasonably effective means to the end that justifies its existence. To be a "reasonably effective means," the power that the clause conveys must be placed in hands that can exercise it when needed and as needed—as needed to advance the end that explains its existence. Lincoln's point was that while a legislature can sometimes act with sufficient resolve and dispatch, it can't always do so, and a power adequate to the public safety must therefore authorize independent executive action as needed. A law that defeats the end that justifies it is to that extent no law, and, analytically, one can't have a legal duty in the absence of a law. Under the circumstances, therefore, Lincoln had a duty to construe the writ suspension clause as he did and ignore Taney's attempt to drain the clause of power adequate to its purpose. No less applies to the framers. If the members of the Philadelphia Convention mistakenly vested the writ suspension power exclusively in incompetent hands, Lincoln did them a favor by disregarding this aspect of their intent, for by doing so he imparted sense to the law, saving it as law, and saving the members of the convention as competent framers of law.

Farber draws a larger moral from Lincoln's action. Though it may seem that Lincoln violated the rule of law in order to save the legal system as a whole, says Farber, the rule of law is flexible enough to admit a role for the personal qualities needed to meet forces that can overwhelm a legal system. "[A]t least in times of crisis," says Farber, "maintaining the ideals of the rule of law depends in a crucial way on the character and courage of a society's leaders."[14] If Lincoln's presidency proves anything, it proves the truth of Farber's conclusion: constitutional maintenance depends on competent and courageous political leadership. Yet Farber doesn't go far enough; he neglects important implications of his position. To begin with, he neglects the fact that "leaders" implies "followers." If the country needs courageous leaders, it needs followers who can recognize and reward courage, or who can be brought to do so, and who to some extent therefore possess this virtue themselves, if only potentially. Farber is also silent about the dispositional nature of character. Neither courage nor any other virtue springs into existence when crises occur; virtues are dispositions that preexist the occasions of their exercise. If the rule of law can't survive without courageous leadership in times of crisis, then it can't survive without leaders who, in normal times, have it in them to act courageously as needed. Nor can it survive without a population that, in normal times, is disposed to recognize and reward courage when events demand it. Such a population would recognize this need and do what it could to provide for it in advance of its need. All this goes to suggest a paradox of political life, namely, that a government that's too successful in providing security and prosperity is risking a complacency of mind and a softness of spirit that are fatal to the virtues that survival demands.

Farber says "dumb luck" as much as anything else "placed Lincoln in the White House" and that "to expect another Lincoln would be foolish."[15] Farber made this judgment in 2003, and the nation's condition in that year could well explain his pessimism. The party of Lincoln had become the party of Reagan and the White South; an unelected president sat in the White House thanks to a party that was no longer willing to accept the outcome of constitutional processes; starve-the-beast tax cuts had killed hopes for investments in the nation's future; and the public had been duped (and a cowardly Congress snookered) into an unjust war with staggering costs to the nation's power and image. No reasonable observer would quarrel with Farber's pessimism then or now. But Farber's despair of another Lincoln is not a judgment that should sit easily with Americans generally or with writers on constitutional matters. As a scholar and teacher of American law, Farber can't practice his profession without some hope, however slim, for the survival of the rule of law in general and American constitutionalism in particular. But how much hope could Farber have if he really believed that constitutional survival depended on a kind of leadership that has long disappeared from the nation's horizon, that almost certainly won't appear again, that probably wouldn't be recognized if it did appear, and whose appearance in any case could be no more than a matter of dumb luck? As evident as these propositions might be, neither Farber nor his readers can accept them without deep regret and at least some resistance. Their falsity or at least the possibility of their falsity must be assumed if the practice of constitutional theory is to serve a practical point.

In this connection it's worth noting that Lincoln may have

disagreed about the role of dumb luck in his own story. Lincoln reached the rhetorical high point of his July 4th message to Congress with his famous declaration about the war's chief aim: "This is a People's contest . . . a struggle for maintaining in the world, that form, and substance of government, whose leading object is, to elevate the condition of men—to lift artificial weights from all shoulders—to clear the paths of laudable pursuit for all—to afford all, an unfettered start, and a fair chance, in the race of life." Prefacing this declaration, Lincoln said, with pride: "It may be affirmed, without extravagance, that the free institutions we enjoy, have developed the powers, and improved the condition, of our whole people, beyond any example in the world. Of this we now have a striking, and an impressive illustration. So large an army as the government has now on foot, was never before known, without a soldier in it, but who had taken his place there, of his own free choice. But more than this: there are many single regiments whose members, one and another, possess full practical knowledge of all the arts, sciences, professions, and whatever else, whether useful or elegant, is known in the world; and there is scarcely one, from which there could not be selected, a President, a Cabinet, a Congress, and perhaps a Court, abundantly competent to administer the government itself."[16]

Might Lincoln have meant a president competent in crises like the one he faced? It's at least possible. It's also possible that he meant a people sufficiently competent to recognize and follow competent leadership, for, he added, "the plain people understand, and appreciate" that this is a contest for "maintaining in the world" that government "whose leading object is, to elevate the condition of [all] men." And while great honor was due to those officers who had remained loyal to the cause of that government, said Lincoln, "the greatest honor, and most important fact of all, is the unanimous firmness, of the common soldiers and common sailors," not one of whom "is known to have deserted his flag. . . . They understand, without an argument, that destroying the government, which was made by Washington, means no good to them."[17]

The moral of Lincoln's presidency thus extends beyond—indeed, far beyond—the need for courageous leaders in times of crisis. The virtues adequate to crises must preexist the crises and characterize the community at large, followers as well as leaders, the many (the "most important fact of all") not just one or a few. Farber missed this larger message, but he can hardly be faulted for that. His implicit hope for the country's survival is undermined enough by his pessimism about another Lincoln. The full implications of Lincoln's presidency, as sketched here, might kill hope altogether, and you can't blame Farber for reluctance to face the abyss. This brings us to a final reservation about Farber's treatment of Lincoln. Though Farber rightly emphasizes Lincoln's moral courage and political skill, he neglects Lincoln's magnanimity, probably because of Farber's own stake in the rule of law and the ways in which a magnanimous attitude toward others clashes with the egalitarian assumptions of the rule of law.

In an oft-cited observation, William Herndon, Lincoln's law partner and biographer, remarked that Lincoln "was always calculating, and always planning ahead" in pursuit of his political ambition, "a little engine that knew no rest."[18] Harry Jaffa, the leading interpreter of Lincoln's thought, joins others who believe that Lincoln included himself when, two decades before the war, he described democracy's biggest threat as the "towering genius" of a Caesar or a Napoleon who "thirsts and burns for distinction" and would have it "whether at the expense of emancipating slaves, or

enslaving free men." These towering men, said Lincoln in his famous "Lyceum Speech" of 1838, belong to "the family of the lion"
and "the tribe of the eagle." They "[m]ost certainly . . . cannot"
find "gratification . . . in supporting and maintaining an edifice
that has been erected by others." Far greater than Herndon's "little
engine," these lion-like ambitions gaze "beyond a seat in Congress,
a gubernatorial or a presidential chair."[19] Yet if Lincoln was indeed
a man of monumental ambition, and if he had an early sense of his
greatness, he, unlike Caesar and Napoleon, did try to "support[]
and maintain an edifice . . . erected by others." Maybe Lincoln saw
this edifice as a platform for his greatness and sought to preserve
the edifice solely as a platform. Though Lincoln denied this charge,
let's leave the question to his biographers and take him at face value
for argument's sake. Whatever his motive for trying to save the edifice, he still saw the edifice as dedicated to the well-being of others.[20] And if, as Jaffa maintains, truly superior persons can have no
real obligation to their inferiors (or if those who feel truly superior
can accept no obligation to their putative inferiors), then Lincoln's
effort to save the edifice must be called an act of magnanimity—
magnanimity as distinguished from, though not always opposed to,
obligation or duty.[21] The safest conclusion is that Lincoln's attitude
toward the Constitution was mixed: he willingly, perhaps magnan-
imously, labored to restore the conditions for constitutional government; he did so maybe because he found pride or saw honor
in doing so.[22] But he may also have felt that he had acquired by
oath a duty to make the effort, as he indicated throughout his first
inaugural address and his July 4th message to Congress.[23] Here,
again, we find an attitude mixed of aspiration and obligation, with
aspiration on top.

Madison on Constitutional Maintenance

We have seen that Madison believed that the first stage of a constitution's development is a special moment; it features initiatives,
relationships, and attitudes that go beyond authorized actions, formal institutions, and a sense of legal obligation. But the founding
is a moment that precedes acts of constitutional maintenance, and
Madison's position on the attitudes and relationships requisite to
constitutional maintenance is unclear. In the 10th and 51st papers
of *The Federalist* he set forth his famous theory of checks and balances as a substitute for statesmanship and patriotic citizenship.
Yet elsewhere in *The Federalist* he relied on attitudes and competences that seem close to statesmanship and patriotic citizenship.
We find more of the same in his call at the conclusion of his presidency for the establishment of a national university, "as a monu-
ment of [Congress's] solicitude for the advancement of knowledge,
without which the blessings of liberty can not be fully enjoyed
or long preserved." Madison envisioned this university as one of
many, "a model instructive" for institutions in the states. More than
a training site for the federal service, it was to attract "youth and
genius from every part of their country, diffusing on their return
examples of those national feelings, those liberal sentiments, and
those congenial manners which contribute cement to our Union
and strength to the great political fabric of which that is the foundation."[24] This great political fabric was, of course, the Constitution. And so in 1815 Madison maintained that the Constitution's
foundation was not self-interest or even enlightened self-interest
but a union of sentiment, and that the government should make
this union of sentiment part of its active concern.[25]

Madison had said essentially the same thirty years before. In

Federalist 14 he appealed to "so many chords of affection" and "the kindred blood that flows in the veins of American citizens," blood whose shedding had "consecrate[ed] their union" (14:88). And on several occasions during the founding period he had proposed a national university to strengthen this foundation. The first of these occasions was in August 1787 when he and Charles Pinckney asked the Philadelphia Convention to grant Congress authority to establish a national university in the nation's capital. Later Madison joined George Washington's call for a national university. On the whole, therefore, Madison's position on constitutional maintenance was a mixture of checking and balancing self-interested behavior *and* cultivating a devotion to public purposes and America as exemplar to the world of government by reflection and choice. Yet the Convention silently tabled the proposed university for reasons that probably included reservations about the scope of national power vis-à-vis the states and misgivings about what would be a secular rival to institutions in the states that were then sponsored by various religious denominations.[26] The proposal's failure left checks and balances as the sole official method of constitutional maintenance.

Checks and balances followed naturally from the view of human nature set forth in *Federalist* 10. Though, said Madison, communities divided regularly along religious and ideological lines, the "most common and durable source of faction" (and in that sense therefore the strongest, the one with the most staying power) "has been the various and unequal distribution of property" (10:59). This was good news because however much a person might want the whole loaf, economic rationality made half a loaf better than none, while the same didn't hold for religious and ideological commitments; compromise could be fatal to them. Political salvation thus

lay in diverting people's energy from religious and ideological beliefs to private economic pursuits that were at once more seductive
to most people most of the time and politically more manageable.
Human nature being what it is, government didn't have to educate
people to the rewards of material gain. Constitution makers had
only to separate church and state, raise the social status of gain, and
attend to the "principle task of modern legislation," which was reg-
ulating economic activity (10:59). This plan called for a sufficiently
large number of economic interest groups to lessen the chances of
majority coalitions on unjust principles and false beliefs; hence the
Large Commercial Republic and, as Madison put it in *Federalist* 51,
a "policy of supplying by opposite and rival interests, the defect of
better motives" (51:349). The "defect" Madison referred to was the
defect of statesmanship and citizenship, the defect of leaders and
followers who wanted to be what *Federalist* 1 assumed the founding generation wanted to be: an exemplar of self-government to
the world (1:3). Madison predicted the decline of this spirit. As the
memory of the Revolution faded, he said in *Federalist* 49, so would
that "enthusiastic confidence of the people in their patriotic leaders, which stifled the ordinary diversity of opinion on great national
questions" and made the Founding possible (49:340–341).

Yet Madison was far from thinking that statesmanship and citizenship would disappear from the new republic. To the contrary,
throughout *The Federalist*, Madison and Hamilton assumed the
active presence of a competent public-spiritedness in every institution of the proposed system, including the various electorates.
One argument for the largeness of the Large Commercial Republic
was that a large population offered voters a choice of more candi-
dates "who possess the most attractive merit, and the most diffusive
and established characters" (10:63). This "chosen body of citizens"

would in turn "refine and enlarge the public views" and thus approximate "the true interests of their country" (10:62). In *Federalist* 57, whose subject is the House of Representatives, Madison said that the first aim of every constitution ought to be the recruitment of such virtuous and capable officials, "and in the next place, to take the most effectual precautions for keeping them virtuous" (57:384). Chief among these precautions was "the vigilant and manly spirit which animates the people of America"; presumably, this spirit would not depart altogether as memory of the Revolution faded (4:387). Madison organized his five papers on the Senate (nos. 62–66) to highlight the ways in which the Senate would provide the government with qualities that the House alone could not provide. Legislators who were older (at least thirty, not twenty-five), elected by a more selective method (by the state legislatures, not ordinary citizens), elected for a longer term of office (six years, not just two), and charged with added responsibilities (confirming treaties and presidential appointments) would be more mature, smarter, more concerned with the nation's image abroad, and withal more responsible.

By "responsible" Madison meant answerable not only *to* public opinion but also—and more importantly—*for* the efficient and fair pursuit of constitutional ends. When "the people . . . call for measures which they themselves will afterwards be the most ready to lament and condemn . . . how salutary will be the interference of some temperate and respectable body of citizens, in order to check the misguided career, and to suspend the blow meditated by the people against themselves, until reason, justice, and truth can be gain their authority over the public mind?" Had the government of Athens "contained so provident a safeguard," the people of Athens "might then have escaped the indelible reproach of decreeing to the

same citizens, the hemlock on one day, and statutes on the next"
(63:425). This well-known passage conceives responsible leadership
as both courageous and educative; it also assumes an educable public. The leaders stand against unjust or unwise public demands and
turn public opinion around. The same picture occurs in *Federalist*
71, where Hamilton claimed that a four-year term would enable a
president to stand against a people whose temporary inclination
diverged from its true interests, "giv[ing] them time and opportunity for more cool and sedate reflection." "Instances might be
cited," said Hamilton, "in which a conduct of this kind has saved
the people from very fatal consequences of their own mistakes, and
has procured lasting monuments of their gratitude to the men, who
had courage and magnanimity enough to serve them at the peril of
their displeasure" (71:482–483).

Madison was aware of a tension between his concern for leadership with special moral qualities and the central part of his constitutional theory, the idea that private incentives could be artfully
arranged to serve public purposes. "It may be suggested," he said
in *Federalist* 63, "that a people spread over an extensive region, cannot like the crowded inhabitants of a small district, be subject to
the infection of violent passions; or to the danger of combining in
the pursuit of unjust measures." This, indeed was what he tried to
show "in a former paper," namely, *Federalist* 10. Yet "this advantage" (of a large territory and a large number of interests) did not
"supersed[e] the use of auxiliary precautions." In fact, "the same
extended situation" that obstructed injustice might in turn force
the country to "remain[] for a longer time, under the influence of
those misrepresentations which the combined influence of [self-]
interested men may succeed in distributing among them" (63:426–
427). Madison thus held that checks and balances alone could not

supply "the defect of better motives" and that the country would need those better motives. It is in this light that the full significance of the proposal for a national university appears. In contrast to any expectation (like the one Diamond was to allege) that a national character would emerge without deliberate educative efforts on the government's part, and notwithstanding the Convention's refusal of authority for such an effort, Madison persisted. Some thirty years after the Founding, and some fifteen years after the Republican revolution of 1800, he urged Congress to establish a public institution to spread liberal and nationalizing sentiments—an institution paid for by taxes on everyone, including antiliberals, and authorized, so he assumed, by Congress's plenary power over the District of Columbia.

Despite his major thrust, Madison agreed with a tenet of political thought that stretched from Plato and Aristotle to Montesquieu and the Antifederalists. These thinkers held that no formal institutions could compensate for the defect of better motives and that successful regimes actively cultivate better motives or civic virtues.[27] Aristotle maintains that a viable constitutional arrangement must reflect the personal commitments of a community's politically most powerful element (Politics, 1310 a–b). In America's case, this would mean one of two things: either a public generally devoted to public purposes or a public that, though devoted to private pursuits, could nevertheless generate, recruit, and vest its trust in public-spirited leaders. In a pluralist system (justified, again, not by calculations of what best serves individual preferences—pluralism or diversity as an end in itself—but by public purposes conceived as real ends to be pursued by fallible actors—pluralism or diversity as instrumental to truth) the leaders in question would comprise a leadership stratum composed of parts (not blindly ideological parties) whose disagreements remained civil from a mutual sense of each other's good faith. The present likelihood of such a regime in America is altogether visionary. This is bad news in light of Madison's ultimate agreement with the Aristotelian tradition about good government without "better motives": it's impossible. Madison acknowledged as much throughout *The Federalist* and on those several occasions of his career when he proposed a national university. In this respect, Madison remained true to his Federalist beginnings. "All of the Federalists' desires to establish a strong and respectable nation in the world," says Gordon Wood, "all of their plans to create a flourishing commercial economy, in short, all of what the Federalists wanted out of the new national government seemed in the final analysis dependent upon the prerequisite maintenance of aristocratic politics."[28] This dependence on "aristocratic politics" influenced the Federalists' conception not only of constitutional success but of constitutionalism itself. "Since," Wood adds, "the Federalists presumed that only such a self-conscious elite could transcend the many narrow and contradictory interests inevitable in any society, however small, the measure of good government became its capacity for insuring the predominance of these kinds of natural leaders who knew better than the people as a whole what was good for society." And the framers' confidence in this "elitist theory of democracy" resulted in their "amazing display of confidence in constitutionalism" itself, which was "the efficacy of institutional devices for solving social and political problems."[29]

Support for the traditional emphasis on attitudes and civic virtues comes from numerous other sources, including three of Hamilton's arguments in *The Federalist*. He defended the Electoral College as the method most likely to fill the presidency with "characters pre-eminent for ability and virtue" (68:461). He argued that

presidential appointment and Senate confirmation is best "calculated . . . to produce a judicious choice of men for filling the offices
of the Union" (76:510). And he predicted that while life-tenured
federal judges would resist violations of the Constitution "instituted by the major voice of the community," the ultimate security
for individual rights would depend not on judicial fortitude and
formal constitutional declarations, but "on public opinion, and on
the general spirit of the people and of the government" (78:528;
84:580). In his "Farewell Address," George Washington called
on the government to "[p]romote . . . institutions for the general
diffusion of knowledge" as "essential" where "a government gives
force to public opinion." Jefferson, another supporter of a national
university, hoped that the University of Virginia could serve in
place of that institution.[30] And beyond the founding era, major
figures and scholars of American political history held from the
early nineteenth century to the present that, in Stephen Macedo's
words, the nation's political order depends "on the habits, values,
and interests formed in 'private' communities, including religious
communities," and that the "support that these communities provide for our shared political project is a vital public concern."[31] The
chief expression of this "vital public concern" has been the public
school movement pioneered by Horace Mann in the early nineteenth century and carried forward into the twentieth century by
John Dewey and others. For both Mann and Dewey, and for most
if its history, this movement has had civic education as its principal
aim.[32] This movement has always had its critics, some justifiable,
some not. Nineteenth- and early-twentieth-century Catholics opposed the use of mandatory public schools as a deliberate means
of weakening the Catholic Church in America.[33] In more recent
times "school choice" has served as cover for resistance to racial

integration and scientific theories that conflict with the Bible.[34] A recent writer has criticized the lasting influence of Mann's emphasis on civic education as inconsistent with an emphasis on individual autonomy and intellectual development demanded by democratic theory, as the writer understands it.[35] Whatever the merits of the public school movement, its long and continuing duration as a force of American life reinforces the history of the Founding and constitutional logic in support of an attitudinal conception of the American regime and therewith an attitudinal theory of constitutional failure and success.

But Not Entirely Attitudinal

Mostly attitudinal doesn't mean entirely attitudinal, however. True, a people that aspired to lead the world by example might produce communities of honest scientists that it might consult on such problems as the role of human activity in the earth's climate change, and this might lead at least to agreement on whether the problem is amenable to human address. This same people might turn to the human and moral sciences to discover what the effect of a growing income gap on equal opportunity and upward mobility and how public policy might address this problem consistently with defensible commitments to parental rights, private property, and due process. But answers from academic sources and special commissions of independent experts will count for naught if they must be processed through policy mechanisms whose many veto points effectively push the threshold of action toward unanimity and the concurrence of the community's least competent and most self-serving elements. Government presupposes that people need government, that they aren't angels, that some simply won't listen,

CONSTITUTIONAL FAILURE 107

and that those who won't listen must be (because they can only be) moved by force alone. A constitution that gives or permits vetoes to Senate and House leaders, individual senators exercising "holds" on legislation or appointments, committee and subcommittee chairpersons, minorities of both houses of Congress (under present rules, 41 in the Senate and 114 in the House), a president, and 5 members of the Supreme Court—such a constitution risks giving vetoes to people who won't listen. The success of such a constitution falls under Daniel Farber's dumb luck category, and luck eventually runs out.

The framers sought to buy time by providing for constitutional change. But Article V is a clear mistake, born of sectional divisions that were too strong for civil war to overcome and put beyond either cure or evasion by growing economic and moral divisions. Though Article V is better than Article XIII was, it's hardly better by much. It gives a veto to as few as fourteen states, representing less than one-tenth of the nation's population. Article V's guarantee that no state can unwillingly lose its equal representation in the Senate gives less than 2 percent of the nation's population the right to perpetuate the present outsized advantage of rural and small-town America in policy decisions, elections, and appointments of a government that is supposed to represent a people whose great majority (80 percent) live in urban centers. Even if 98 percent of the country should awaken to the need to change the Senate's apportionment, change could not come through the "legal" machinery, and extralegal change like that of the Founding and Reconstruction is ruled out by its unbearable economic consequences.[36] This system must eventually fail the test for constitutional success: a politics that offers realistic hope for reasonable progress toward "the real welfare of the great body of the people."

I've argued that the Constitution's preamble and amending rule jointly imply that a healthy politics is the Constitution's leading object. From this it follows that the Constitution assumes that all permanent elements of the community are capable of participating in a healthy politics, as either leaders or followers. But a healthy politics can be no more than an aspiration, for because government is coercive government, it assumes that some in the community are beyond the reach of evidence and logic. The best anyone can hope for is a tolerable approximation of a healthy politics. Assessments of the Constitution's prospects will therefore vary with assessments of how far the nation is from a healthy politics—how far constitutional processes are from producing reasonably tolerable policies and electoral results.

A nation approaches constitutional failure when significant factions deny that adherence to constitutional processes is consistent with acceptable outcomes. Those who expect the worst from constitutional processes have reason to obstruct their operation and refuse cooperation with their electoral and policy results. This is where the nation is now, or so Republican reaction to the Obama presidency indicates. Beyond the advent of the Hastert Rule of the House Republican Caucus and the escalation of the Senate filibuster to a routine tactic, examples of this reaction include voter suppression laws in some thirty states as of January 2012.[37] Harvey Mansfield has been remarkably candid about the thinking behind these measures. Unlike his fellow right-wingers with their dishonest cries of "voter fraud," Mansfield rises with boldness to assert that voting in the true sense must be informed voting and that no informed American would have voted for Barack Obama and the European socialism that his party seeks.[38] Because we can expect an equally toxic reaction from progressive Democrats if and when the voters elect a Republican president, American politics may well remain dysfunctional long past the time available to cope with global warming and avoid fiscal collapse, permanent underclasses, and an oligarchy that can govern only through fraud and violence.

5

Constitutional Reform and Constitutional Thought

Whether a constitution (a government under a constitution) works to approximate goods like security and prosperity depends on historical conditions that fall beyond human capacity to control or predict. For this reason a successful constitution will contain provisions for constitutional criticism and change. These provisions for change are tools. As tools, they should be tailored for the people who are to use them. A constitution made for Americans should enable Americans to pursue constitutional ends, the real goods that the constitution is supposed to be an instrument of. Instrumental constitutions thus presuppose morally and intellectually competent agents. Where the agent is "the sovereign people," and where the aims are real goods, provisions for constitutional change presuppose a nation that can alter its government not just when it wants to, but when it should—that is, when the government fails over an extended period of time to maintain or make reasonable progress toward its ends. This conclusion reflects the U.S. Constitution's nature as an instrument not just for aggregating popular preferences, but for enhancing chances that popular government will do the right thing—that, more often than not, popular government will try to serve the public's true interests in a manner that respects individual and minority rights. Walter Murphy thus concluded that the preeminent constitutional virtue is not fidelity to a given constitution but the moral and intellectual capacity to make and reform constitutions. Murphy called those who recognized the need for this virtue *constitutionalists*; he called those who venerated particular constitutions *constitutionists*. By the Constitution's instrumental logic, a constitution that leaves its people incapable of constitutional reform—a constitution that fosters constitutionism at the expense of constitutionalism—is a failure in progress.[1]

Other writers who have elevated constitution making over constitutional fidelity include Louis Michael Seidman, Jack Balkin, and Sanford Levinson. I'll comment on Balkin and Levinson later in this chapter. Seidman has gone as far as to deny the Constitution's obligatory force and summon Americans to resume their forefathers' constitution-making character, outside Article V. Seidman calls for limited change, not change across the board. He would preserve commitments to democracy and equality, separated institutions, and basic political and personal freedoms.[2] But how he would peacefully change the "grotesquely malapportioned Senate," the Electoral College, and other "pernicious provisions," he doesn't say. Nor does he justify his optimism that social and economic upheaval would not accompany change through the "constitutional disobedience" that he advocates. True, as Seidman emphasizes, unlawful change has happened before, in the late 1780s and the mid-1860s; he says it must soon happen again if Americans are to redeem their claim to be a self-governing people.[3]

But that the country can have yet another rebirth of reason is a distant hope in this era of ideological division and the profound dependencies and vulnerabilities wrought by modern technology. No modern democracy could tolerate the protracted economic disruption that would follow a serious move toward unauthorized change of constitutional structures. Seidman is surely right to say that "before abandoning our heritage of self-government, we ought to try extricating ourselves from constitutional bondage so that we can give real freedom a chance."[4] But this exhortation amounts to a conditional proposition, "if not x, then y," and no degree of aversion to y can guarantee x. If by constitutional reform we mean voluntary constitutional reform, foreseeable conditions in America make constitutional reform on any meaningful scale a pipedream. This is especially the case if the root of America's institutional problems is a sick politics. If institutional problems in America are symptomatic of cultural problems, then constitutional reform must reach beyond governmental institutions to the character of American life and political culture. Hope for constitutional reform is thus hope that the nation can change the way Americans taken at random see their responsibilities to anonymous others, present and future. Seidman is aware—indeed, he emphasizes—that cultural change must precede constitutional change.[5] He knows that cultural change is connected to "broad social, material, and economic forces" that aren't easily redirected. He knows that the nation's cultural divisions run deep ("all the way to the bottom," he says at one point) and that as "middle ground" recedes "out of reach," Americans have "lost the tools for disagreeing agreeably."[6] Despite all this, however, Seidman finds "reasons for optimism." These reasons seem to be three in number: the election of a black president, the recent victories of the gay rights movement, and "a hunger" among "[m]any Americans" for ending a politics "that demonizes opponents and makes compromise impossible."[7] Yet even if Seidman has evidence for this last of his "reasons for optimism," none of these reasons comes even close to the breadth and intensity of popular feeling that it would take for needed structural changes. At this writing the many Americans who supported Barack Obama and who support gay marriage have yet to constitute a political force sufficient to deprive the American Right of its veto in the U.S. Senate, much less its veto under Article V. Structural change of any consequence seems all but impossible by lawful means absent internal collapse (like the Civil War and the Great Depression) or cataclysmic shock from outside (Pearl Harbor or worse). Seidman's optimism must be due to more than he reveals, and until he and other optimists offer more, one can doubt the nation's capacity for serious constitutional reform. Certain it is that major institutional change under Article V is virtually impossible. If change depends on Article V—if Americans (and foreigners invested in America) don't acknowledge and act on historical precedents (like the Civil War Amendments) for bypassing Article V, the Constitution of 1789 is a dead man walking.

The nation's apparent loss of constitutionalist capacity confronts the American legal academy with a dilemma. American constitutional scholars have an obligation to the community that supports them. In the abstract, this obligation is an obligation to return good for good. Though no one will deny this general obligation, its specifics are difficult to describe. One can't know what good to return until one knows the condition of the community to which one is obligated. One would hardly be obligated to return a borrowed shotgun to its owner at the moment of her drunken threat to shoot an unfaithful partner. But what about an obligation to tell the truth to a dying man when no further good could come of it?

Constitutional scholars are part of the scientific community, which is part of the larger civic community. As the civic community sees its relationship to the scientific community, the civic community pays the scientific community to seek and tell the truth. A scientist who lies is no scientist insofar as she lies. A scientist as scientist therefore must tell a dying man the truth even if no further good comes of it. Yet if no further good comes of it, a man comfortable with illusions might just as soon not know he's dying. Suppose the dying man is himself something of a scientist, however; suppose he defines himself as devoted above all to a life of "reflection and choice" and, as a reflective person, fears above all else "the lie in the soul." This man would have a mixed identity: part comfortable with illusion, part wanting the truth. What's best for this man under the circumstances? And what is the obligation of the citizen-scientist in this circumstance? This is the question facing constitutional scholarship in America today. What can constitutional scholars responsibly do or say when there's nothing to do or say that isn't harmful to the country in some way? What can constitutional scholars do or say when the nation's loss of constitutionalist capacity leaves the survival of constitutional government to Dumb Luck or Divine Grace?

I see no way out of this dilemma except by denying (pretending to deny?) its predicate: the hopeless state of constitutional government in America. Maybe one can say with Hamilton that the aspiration to government by reflection and choice is universal with mankind and that it will resurface with sufficient force at some future time, perhaps even in America itself. If that time should arrive, future constitution makers might profit from knowledge of what went wrong with the experiment of 1789. If I were compelled to guess what went wrong I'd seek the philosophic sources of obvious mistakes like the idea that a consumer culture could support a good government, the related idea that checks and balances could "supply the defect of better motives," and the rejection by Congress and the Philadelphia Convention of Madison's call for a national university. I'd look for the sources of these errors in America's colonial experience and ultimately in what Jacob Klein described as the "Protagorean fascination" (the belief that "man is the measure of all things") behind the shift from ancient to modern ideas of freedom and science.[8] But this book ventures no such hypothesis. In this concluding chapter I comment only on the immediate obstacles to successful thought about what went wrong and what to do at some future point well beyond anything we have reason to expect.

Some of these obstacles are too obvious for extended commentary. This category includes politicized religious zeal, a fact made relevant to the present discussion by the power of the Religious Right in the Republican Party. Religious thought understands itself as dependent ultimately on faith. Religious faith is faith in God's love of man, something man can't understand because man's finite mind can't comprehend the infinite mind of God. The believer's life is thus grounded in something he can't understand or even, on pain of impiety, try to understand. The believer in the biblical god has to believe that what amounted to Eve's original decision to think for herself instead of blindly obeying the command of her creator was the most disastrous of human events. But who can understand the opening chapters of Genesis? Why God programmed the first humans to desire autonomous knowledge and then punished them and their progeny for acting on this desire is certainly a mystery of the Creation. Yet many true believers base their lives on this mystery. They would see Aristotle's observation that all men desire to know—the desire to know about everything, including the most important things—as confirming the desire of all men to sin. Believers strive for a life of obedience instead, or so they say. But even if *all* men don't desire to know, the desire to know independently of divine revelation has gripped many men and women from the days of Eden to the present. And we seem stuck with the fact that over the last four centuries a desire for autonomous knowledge has steadily overpowered contrary religious impulses in every part of the world except sections of the Mideast. The American constitutional experience is part of this development.

What holds for religion, however, holds also for dogmatic beliefs of all stripes, including the maxims of free-market capitalism and constitutional doctrines like "limited government" and the so-called wall separating church and state. A dogma is a dogma; it marks the place where thought gives way to thoughtless execution. The doctrinaire or unreflective application of constitutional maxims leads to indefensible results and obscures the fact that the "rule of law" must find accommodation with the need for prudential leadership, especially in times of crisis, when law runs out, as the Founding and Lincoln's presidency should have proved to all Americans.[9] Regarding the separation of church and state, for example, a truly impenetrable wall would effectively outlaw not only faith-based enemies of liberal democracy but faith-based friends of liberal democracy, to no good end save furtherance of the self-defeating myth of liberal neutrality toward religion.[10] The same holds for "limited government." In the Supreme Court's recent decision in the Health Care Case a doctrinaire understanding of "limited government" yielded the astonishing conclusion that, even absent questions involving individual rights, Congress cannot use its commerce power to address in an admittedly reasonable way what all sides acknowledge to be a national economic problem of great magnitude.[11]

Constitution worship (Murphy's "constitutionism") is the biggest obstacle to successful thought about the Constitution's problems. Chapter 1 of this book shows how constitution worship forces people to falsify both moral and material reality. Constitution worship would therefore make sense mostly to two kinds of people: those who affirm against all evidence that mankind makes its own moral and material reality, and those whose incapacity to deal with reality makes them vulnerable to political manipulation under color of law. This is not necessarily to condemn manipulation under color of law, for that may be the best arrangement for people who can't handle the truth. Think of the Founding, the Louisiana Purchase, the Civil War and Reconstruction, cases like *Home Building and Loan Assn. v. Blaisdell* (1941) and *Bush v. Gore* (2000), and maybe even the current war against jihadist Islam. In each of these situations agencies of government acted (or are acting) unconstitutionally—and "saved" (are saving) the Constitution in the process, at least as far as the general public is concerned.[12] Madison himself signaled approval of such political manipulation when he said in *Federalist* 49 that the most rational constitution will need the prejudices of the community on its side. Think of what Madison's statement could mean. The most rational constitution would be a constitution that worked most of the time but not all of the time, for no constitution can work all the time. In other words, the best constitution could only be the best *feasible* constitution under the circumstances. It might be well for the public to believe that this best of feasible constitutions is working on those occasions when it isn't working, lest a moment of disappointment be followed by overreach and the installation of a worse constitution over the best that the nation is currently capable of. Yet another occasion for falsifying reality to people who couldn't face the truth would be, as I've noted, when a constitution falls into irreversible decline.

In any case, constitutionalists (as opposed to constitutionists) must count constitution worship a vice because it defeats prospects for government by reflection and choice. In fact, constitution worship doesn't really work even for constitutionists; constitution worship is a vice even from its own perspective of fidelity to law. Fidelity to the Constitution as written would entail reaffirming the Constitution's claim to be an instrument of its ends, and one could not reaffirm that claim without subjecting it to a critical examination that constitution worship precludes.[13] Constitution worship is generally the anticonstitutional vice of the American Right, which, roughly since the deaths of Martin Diamond and Herbert Storing in 1977, has tended to downplay the Constitution's defects and portray critics of the Constitution from the Progressive Era to the present as lacking either in patriotism or gratitude.[14] An important exception to this pattern is Francis Fukuyama. In a book in press at this writing, Fukuyama argues persuasively that the Constitution is in decline that can be reversed probably by nothing short of another Great Depression or Civil War, and that much of the fault lies with the number of veto points in the original design stemming from distrust of executive government and presently exacerbated by ideological division.[15] The remaining obstacles to an understanding of constitutional failure are intellectual vices mostly of the establishment center-left, namely, value-neutrality and historicism. Before we examine these obstacles to constitutional thought, I remind the reader of what we're looking for and why.

Right Answers, Anyone?

Makers of a democratic constitution envision government that justifies its conduct to the general public in terms of goods that the public can understand (prosperity, security, fairness) and the institutions for pursuing these goods. For this reason constitutional democracy can obtain only among those who agree on (1) what kind of things are worth securing through coercion (coercion because it's government we're discussing) and (2) what counts as evidence of truth about means *and* about ends. Public reasonableness as a state of affairs assumes people who (at the very least) will listen to each other, and people with irreconcilably different notions of goodness and truth-seeking won't listen to each other. One can't give reasons to someone who doesn't share one's sense of what counts as a reason and how to conduct the process of reasoning together. A population whose major segments won't listen to each other can't constitute one political regime; its segments can't participate in an authority that would justify its conduct to all.

Yet a government that *would* justify its conduct to all is not one that actually succeeds in doing so. In strictness, there can be no government of any size and complexity that actually succeeds in justifying its conduct to all of its people all the time. Government, again, is coercive government, and coercive government presupposes an inclination to disobey. It presupposes a recalcitrance to reason that discursive persuasion can't always reverse—hence, the need for coercion. Justifying coercion to everyone would therefore have to be an aspiration—something government tries, persistently falls short of, yet keeps trying to do. Where this aspiration is held to be compatible with electoral democracy, a constitution must institutionalize criticism of the government at the same time that it tries, through public education (including publically licensed and supported private education) to promote a population whose members can and do respect both each other and the adjudicatory, deliberative, and electoral institutions of public reason. These efforts will fail occasionally given the cultural differences in the populations of modern democracies and, more basically, the variable intellectual, moral, and psychological capacities of the individuals who comprise those populations. But among democrats who retain faith in mass democracy, nonsystemic and occasional failures and merely partial successes won't weaken the faith that men and women taken at random can think straight about the world, if they only will. And since ordinary men and women assume just one world with real moral and nonmoral dimensions, nonsystemic failures shouldn't be enough to defeat the assumption of one workable right answer (or best answer) to every moral issue (like the fairness of the income gap) and nonmoral issue (like the income gap's effect on economic mobility). Even if people in a given case don't agree on what the right answer is, its assumed existence enables them to make sense of what they're doing when they disagree about something—submitting and testing competing versions of a truth that is beyond their making and to which their opinions are responsible. The presumed existence of this truth also influences their thought by defining a range of reasonable alternatives.[16]

These assumptions about truth and the desire and capacity of responsible persons justify coercing persons who violate laws reasonably conducive to the public interest and respectful of human rights. Assume that most people generally want to see and can be brought to see the one right answer to an issue and you enable the educative and regulatory activities of a government that aspires to justify its conduct to all—that is, to all reasonable persons, the only persons to whom anyone owes reasons. The converse is also true: deny right answers, or deny that most people most of the time value right answers *and* can be brought to act on them, *and* act on them in time to meet their opportunities and threats—deny any of these things and you abandon the defense of constitutional democracy. You abandon government by publicly responsible reflection and choice, and you open the way to government by willfulness beyond human understanding, like government by persons who are favored by Fortune (Dumb Luck) or who speak for God.

No Right Answers

In mid-November, 2013, the Boston University School of Law held a two-day conference on the Constitution's involvement in the nation's current political dysfunction. Participants of this conference included many of the continent's top constitutional theorists, names like Michelman, Balkin, Levinson, Tushnet, Greve, Fleming, West, and Hirschel. Yet with one or two exceptions over the course of seven panels and two keynote speeches, none of the many proposals for constitutional reform reached beyond institutional changes to cultivate the patriotism and philanthropy to which Hamilton and Lincoln appealed, one for establishing the Constitution and the other for saving it. Most of the proposals (involving veto points, campaign finance, partisan gerrymandering, at-large elections, proportional representation, etc.) assumed that more democracy was key to reducing the nation's political ills to tolerable levels. Some participants agreed with Thomas Mann and Norman Ornstein, who argue in a recent book that the major cause of the nation's current political dysfunction is the ideological extremism of the modern Republican Party.[17] Several of the participants went beyond what may be transitory to more systemic factors to suggest that the nation's present political dysfunction represents congenital pathologies of modern democracy itself, like the inability of a consumer culture either to avoid problems like global warming and fiscal collapse or to tolerate the long-term sacrifices needed to address such problems.[18]

In the question period of the conference's last session, I spoke from the audience to note the paucity of suggestions for addressing the attitudinal causes of political dysfunction, like the GOP's ideological extremism, and I asked members of the panel whether value-neutrality among academic liberals precluded proposals that might promote a culture of public reasonableness. Sanford Levinson, a panelist and the conference's eminence grise, replied, in effect, yes: liberal constitutionalism does preclude efforts to cultivate liberal attitudes. Levinson cited the opinion of Justice James Clark McReynolds in *Pierce v. Society of Sisters* (1925). In this case the Supreme Court voided an Oregon statute that would have closed the Catholic primary and secondary schools of that state. In his opinion for a unanimous court, McReynolds said that the "fundamental theory upon which all governments in this Union repose excludes any general power of the state to standardize its children by forcing them to accept instruction from public teachers only." "The child is not a mere creature of the state," McReynolds added; "those who nurture him and direct his destiny have the right, coupled with the high duty, to recognize and prepare him for higher obligations."[19] Such was "the doctrine of *Meyer v. Nebraska*," said McReynolds, a case for which he had written the Court's opinion two years earlier. In *Meyer*, the Court voided Nebraska's ban on teaching modern languages other than English in the state's primary schools. While it was "easy to appreciate" the state's "desire . . . to foster a homogeneous people with American ideals prepared readily to understand current discussions of civic matters," the state could not use means that "submerge[d] the individual" in the manner of ancient Sparta and Plato's "Ideal Commonwealth."[20]

By assuming that the message of *Pierce* answered my question, Levinson implied that discouraging ideological extremism is a step toward totalitarianism. If Levinson is right, then liberal constitutionalists can't foster liberal constitutionalism without betraying liberal constitutionalism. There's no telling how many of the conferees agreed with this position, and I'd like to think that no one, including Levinson, really agrees with it. But something has to explain the conference's near silence about what Madison, Jefferson, and Washington saw as the "liberal sentiments" on which constitutional government depends. And Levinson's position at the conference was consistent with the value-neutrality he has expressed elsewhere (though not everywhere),[21] and not inconsistent with the value-neutralism of mainstream political science and academic law.

Earlier that day the BU conferees were treated to a luncheon address by Jack Balkin, titled "The Last Days of Disco." Balkin ingeniously wove the titles of "disco hits" from the 1970s into a message of hope: what seems like dysfunction is actually "transition," and though the transition will be difficult, the country will get through it.[22] Balkin's address was a hit with the audience, an entertaining delivery of a message everyone wanted to hear. But every gathering has its contrarian, and this occasion brought forth confirmation of that truth in the person of Michael Greve. In the discussion period that followed Balkin's address, Greve noted that Balkin had avoided mention of what his vaunted "transition" was a transition to. How, Greve asked, could Balkin be sure that the country was heading for political functionality and not a state of "sheer entropy"? Greve asked this question in view of what he saw as the failure of both major political parties to put forth "some coherent program" for the country's direction. Balkin applauded the question and offered what he seemed to think was an answer. He advised "very careful" study of some "very gauzy terms at the very highest abstraction" in some of President Obama's speeches.[23] By this response, which drew Greve's polite silence, Balkin may have intended to counter Greve's claim that neither political party had a program. But the heart of Greve's question—whether Balkin could justify his optimism—went unanswered.

Not that Balkin hadn't anticipated the question. During his address he had predicted that the Reagan coalition would break up and that the nation's political parties would be more sensitive to the nation's demographic changes. He had also predicted that the parties would rely for cohesion more on data bases than patronage. But he pointedly declined to predict the country's substantive direction. Regarding the current ideological struggle in the United States, he said: "What could happen? We don't really know the answer, but it's very much like watching a fight between two exhausted fighters, neither of which can land a knockout blow." Yet he insisted that the conflict was "the birth pangs of something new."[24] He also insisted that this something new would be something functional.[25] His evidence seemed to be little more than the nation's past: we've come through rough patches before. But, of course, what's happened before, standing alone, is hardly compelling evidence of what will happen again. If surviving past ills guaranteed surviving future ills, virtually no mature person, tribe, or political system would ever die. Balkin had thus anticipated a question for which he had not provided and on this occasion would not provide an answer. Combing the transcript of Balkin's address for possible answers, one finds little more than an expression of faith, delivered in the accents of a rock journalist: "Nevertheless, as Hot Chocolate once brilliantly put it, I believe in miracles and that we will turn the beat around and get ourselves to Funky town. That's the way, uh-huh, uh-huh, I like it, uh-huh, uh-huh. And remember, I close with the words of the great political scientist, Gloria Gaynor, we will survive."[26]

That these responses from Levinson and Balkin met with little criticism from an audience of such high caliber is cause for deepening pessimism for the nation's future. Can it be that at least a generation after their collapse in academic philosophy, historicism and the fact-value dichotomy have lost little of their influence in American political science and academic law? If so, and if I may modify a thought borrowed from Mann and Ornstein, things are indeed much worse than they look. As though the polity's loss of constitutionalist competence were not bad enough, our legal academics—even the best of them—may be unable even to describe, much less confront, the problem of constitutional dysfunction. I say *may* be unable to describe the problem, for Levinson is less than consistently value-neutral, Balkin is less than consistently historicist, and though no voices are as influential in the present discussion as theirs, other voices do exist.

To show why there's cause to regret value-neutrality and historicism, let me reiterate my argument: an ends-oriented constitutionalism is the only constitutionalism that's faithful to the demands of practical reason and the facts of the nation's founding. Actors want only what they believe are real goods, not what they acknowledge to be apparent goods, and mature actors know that they can mistake apparent for real goods and miscalculate the means to real goods. Practical reason therefore counsels self-criticism, openness to opposing views, and a willingness to change one's mind about ends and means. Projected from the plane of individual decision to governmental practice, practical reason counsels institutions for criticizing, and if need be changing, governmental policies and even formal institutions. If the government is a democracy, practical reason counsels institutions for representing, refining, and educating public opinion to its true interest—ultimately the value of self-critical public reason and its associated rights (involving speech, fairness, and property, for example). Though government presupposes that coercion may be necessary, coercion can be justified only if the government has publically shareable evidence to believe that all responsible persons would agree that its policies are reasonable approximations of everyone's true interest. Coercion is justified, in other words, only if the government has reason to believe that in any given circumstance there are demonstrable right or at least better answers to questions of ends and means. Deny that there are right answers and the case for constitutional government collapses and talk of constitutional success becomes meaningless. Balkin's historicism and Levinson's value-neutrality implicitly deny right answers.

Value-Neutral Liberalism

I begin with a matter that's more important than may initially appear: Levinson's misunderstanding of Justice McReynolds's opinion in *Pierce*. Because McReynolds was clear that the decision in *Pierce* fell "[u]nder the doctrine of *Meyer v. Nebraska*," we should construe *Pierce* in light of *Meyer*. Taking both opinions together, we see that McReynolds was far from denying that a liberal regime could legitimately cultivate liberal attitudes. In fact, McReynolds said in *Meyer* "[t]hat the State may do much, go very far, indeed, in order to improve the quality of its citizens, physically, mentally, and morally."[27] What he denied in both cases was that the state could cultivate the virtues of citizenship by any means whatever, like outlawing foreign-language instruction and closing Catholic schools. In this respect McReynolds's opinion was fully consistent with Madison's call for using admitted national power to promote "liberal sentiments," for by no account is liberalism monolingual, and by all accounts liberalism is committed to a reasonable liberty of conscience. Levinson's reading of McReynolds is more Levinson than McReynolds, therefore, and *Pierce* is no authority for Levinson's position. Levinson needs an argument in any case, not a citation, and one is left to guess what that argument might be. The only doctrine that could condemn using state power to foster liberal attitudes would be the morally skeptical claim that all political stances are equally irrational, including the commitment to experiential public reason. If the liberal commitment to experiential reason is arbitrary, then liberalism can have no reason for discouraging beliefs based on dogmas, religious and secular, that experiential reason can't penetrate or confirm, like the sinfulness of science, the subservience of women, the evils of homosexuality, the rising tide, the justice of poverty, and checks and balances in lieu of better motives.

But the response to value-skepticism is older than the hills: If liberalism has no reason for promoting liberalism, it has no reason for *not* promoting liberalism; and skeptics can't coherently object to promoting liberalism for, they say, no one can *reasonably* object (or not object) to anything. Skeptics might reply in turn that, indeed, liberals do have a reason for avoiding antiliberalism: consistency with liberalism itself. But this response would imply what the skeptics themselves would count as a meaningless value judgment coupled with what all must agree is a false sociological premise. The false premise is that there is a consensus definition of liberalism, and the value judgment is that liberals ought to follow that definition. Yet the current debate over the promotion of liberal virtues proves that there is no authoritative conception of liberalism, and even if skeptics could justify their conception of liberalism, they would have to explain how (the value of) consistency with any such conception could be free of the irrationality that skeptics attribute to value judgments generally. Here we must bear in mind that when Levinson suggests that promoting liberalism is either equivalent to totalitarianism or a step toward it, he's denying a rational distinction between superstition, on the one hand, and, on the other hand, a desire for truth from a sense of fallibility and through exchanging reasons based on shareable experience. Deny this distinction and you deny a morally relevant distinction between consistency and inconsistency, for consistency is a value only within the practice of seeking right answers from a sense of fallibility and through exchanging reasons based on shareable experience. (If truth is multiple, not singular, then one truth can deny another truth and both can still be true.) Though I would regard this truth-seeking practice—the reflective, experienced-based quest for right answers—as definitive of humankind, we can safely put aside talk of "humankind," for all will agree that this practice is at least a matter of very deep and long-standing convention among those peoples of the world that are known to American constitutional thought. I mean the "candid World" to which the Declaration of Independence addressed its reasons.

At this point, a thoroughgoing value-skeptic might try to defend Levinson by claiming that moral philosophy has moved beyond the

"natural law," thinking of the eighteenth century. But Levinson
knows better. Despite his skeptical construction of McReynolds's
opinion in *Pierce*, Levinson has acknowledged three crucial facts
that speak against academic value-neutrality and its supporting
metaethics, at least in the field of constitutional commentary: (1)
the widespread popular belief that democracy and justice are real
values;[28] (2) moral realism as an important position in present-day
academic philosophy[29]; and (3) the inability of value-neutral academics to answer normative questions involving constitutional
failure or success.[30]

Levinson himself has made good use of this last point against
political scientists such as David Mayhew and Shep Melnick.
They have argued that despite America's pattern of divided government since the collapse of the postwar consensus in the 1960s,
the national government has been reasonably productive, not "broken," especially in comparison with other Western governments.[31]
Levinson has argued forcefully to the contrary for a decade in two
books and numerous articles that have set the terms of the current discussion and established him as "the unofficial spokesman
for progressive critics of the Constitution"[32] and "America's greatest revolutionary constitutionalist."[33] In response to Mayhew and
Melnick, Levinson notes that government's productivity is partly
a normative question that can't be answered simply by listing "only
titles of bills and the numbers of . . . legislative acts." "The real task
before us," says Levinson, "is . . . rather, to *evaluate* the quality of
the legislation" and to "compare and contrast the rather small set
of bills that are passed against a far larger subset that never had a
chance." "That task," says Levinson, "doesn't fit easily within the
notion of value-free social science."[34]

By this response to Mayhew and Melnick, Levinson does more

than distance himself from value-free social science. He also implies a partially substantive test of constitutional success. The reader will recall the two-part test elaborated in chapter 2: that constitutional success involves (1) public support for (2) progress toward substantive goods understood independently of public opinion. This test reflects a conception of the Constitution as designed to raise public opinion to objective standards of the public interest and individual rights. It differs from the simpler test of public approval and its corresponding conception of the Constitution as an instrument for aggregating popular preferences. Though a social science that was truly value-neutral could have no reason for preferring the simpler test to the two-part test, the simpler test predominates among today's legal academics in law and political science.

As for how to measure public opinion in constitutional context, more would be involved than polling for the public's assessment of government's performance. Where the public had a high opinion of the Constitution, as is presently the case, the public would see the constitutional arrangement of offices and powers as the authoritative instrument for registering public opinion. One could infer, in other words, that as between government by public opinion poll and government by the Constitution's offices and powers, the public would prefer the latter. Whatever the public might say to opinion pollsters from time to time, therefore, the public's continuing support of the Constitution *and* the paucity of challenges to the legal right of officials to their offices, would make "what the government does" maybe not the only index of public opinion but the one that counts for governmental purposes. Moreover, "what the government does," would include what the government decided not to do. What some might see as failure to address, say, global warming or the income gap wouldn't be failure at all if the aggregate of public preferences as processed through the most authoritative process favored the status quo. A focus on quantitative output, like that of Mayhew and Melnick, assumes an aggregate-of-preferences test of governmental performance. But by an aggregate-of-preferences test, approval of the Constitution and acceptance of the commissions of officeholders all but preclude a negative assessment of governmental performance. Whatever the government does or doesn't do reflects the aggregate of preferences. Levinson therefore has good reason for rejecting the Mayhew-Melnick approach, and by doing so he implies a two-part test of the kind elaborated in chapter 2 of this book.

Analysts who apply a two-part test need theories that correspond to the two parts, namely, a theory of constitutional ends and a theory of democratic choice. Levinson has offered no explicit theory either of democratic choice or of constitutional ends. But a theory of democratic choice is implicit in his proposal for a plenary constitutional convention to address the nation's institutional ills. Levinson calls for a two-year convention of delegates to be paid the salary of Supreme Court justices. Selection of these delegates by lottery would protect the convention from the undue influence of "single issue zealots who might, with the support of generous financing, prevail in elections." Delegates would also "operate with a budget sufficient to allow hearings all over the United States and the world that would allow them to make the most informed choices possible."[35] As for the content of these choices, and therewith the ends of constitutional government, Levinson indicates throughout that he speaks not from one or another special interest but from the perspective of a framer who's interested chiefly in the national interest, including the nation's image in the world.[36] From his focus on public goods, Levinson's mode of decision follows. That mode will be public-spirited and scientifically informed deliberation, as distinguished from bargaining by special interests and hostage taking by ideological purists (as in recent congressional battles over raising the national debt-ceiling). Influenced by James Fishkin's "deliberative polling," which he sees as modeled after James Madison's mode of thought, Levinson envisions his constitutional convention as a kind of "deliberative assembly" charged with the nation's most vital interests.[37]

Levinson's occasional view that a liberal government can't promote an attitude of public reasonableness must be weighed against all that he says about the limitations of value-neutrality, the aims of constitutional government, the value of informed and public-spirited deliberation, and the checking of single-issue zealotry in the constitutional convention he calls for. Whatever the balance indicates about the coherence of Levinson's position or his consistency from one occasion to the next, one can safely conclude that he has no argument against Madison's judgment that the survival of a liberal order depends on liberal attitudes and a government that fosters them.

Historicism

By historicism I mean the general view that truth is a matter of perspective that changes from one quantum of time (generation, era, epoch) to the next. Historicists hold that the meaning of ideas like "security," "prosperity," "reason," and a "healthy politics" changes at areas along a time continuum. At one area of the time continuum "reason" might mean consistency with premises whose truth is revealed through clerical authority; at another area of the time continuum the premises might be established by repeatable experiences ("experiments") confirmable in principle by observers taken at random from populations taken at random. One might liken these areas of change to smudges on a never-ending line. This smudge-bedecked line would represent "history," and the smudges on the line would share a property called "historicity." (Lest there be a history of history, history itself would not display the property of historicity; history would be transhistorical.) One might prefer to call the smudges "points" to avoid the awkwardness of "smudge." But "smudge" is the better word. A point doesn't blend into something else the way a smudge does; points don't flow the way lines and smudges do. "Point" connotes discreteness, or boundedness, or separation—all of which are notions that belong to a view of reality as a totality of articulated parts, which parts are different kinds of things, each kind with its own separate and distinct being. What's ordinarily meant by "time" is not like that; like "line" (as opposed to a line segment, a thing that stops at two points, one here, one there), "time" stretches in different directions indefinitely and all at once. Time thus stretches into the past and into the future right now. (Unlike future and past *events*, which don't exist now, *the future* and *the past* exist now; hence, the sense attached to the thought that we have both a past and a future right now.) Since an area of the time line called "today" emerges from "yesterday" and anticipates "tomorrow," "today" looks fore and aft at the same time and is therefore more a smudge than a point. Points as points stand still. Smudges as smudges don't stand still; they smudge because they are no longer smudges at the places where they narrow and blend back into the thin line. Smudges as smudges are transitional, in other words, and *transitional* is an important notion in the present discussion. "Transitional" is Jack Balkin's description of where political America is today (and where it was yesterday and will be tomorrow?).

Like a smudge, an area or a period of transition is hard to de-
lineate (de-line-i-ate) or "point out" or "pin down" with a definite
(a defining, a separating) description. Levinson, Seidman, Mann
and Ornstein, and many other writers use the attribute "broken"
to describe the present state of the nation's political institutions.
"Broken" is reasonably clear because it has an opposite; it means the
opposite of "working" or "functioning." When Levinson and other
writers say the system is broken they mean it isn't working. Balkin
may not be able to say that; at the very least, he's not sure that the
system isn't working. In his address to the BU conference, Balkin
said that in the 1960s and 1970s,

> most people thought the United States was thoroughly
> ungovernable. . . . [N]obody [?!] says that anymore. That is
> to say that there was a previous regime of dysfunction. It was
> also the end of one constitutional regime and the beginning of
> another constitutional regime. And my message for you today
> is simply that: that what looks like constitutional dysfunction
> is actually constitutional transition . . . a movement between
> two constitutional regimes. This particular transition is going
> to be very difficult. . . . But we, in fact, will get through it and
> when we get through it on the other side, it will look quite
> different and people will not, in fact, say we are in a system of
> constitutional dysfunction anymore.[38]

Thus, Balkin won't say "broken." But he also won't say the system
is working. In a way, it seems to be both: not working and working
all at once, or not working on the way to working.

I won't pause to question every part of Balkin's message, but,
like Greve, I would like to know how Balkin can be confident that

the system is in transition to a functional state. If our present state appears to be dysfunctional but really is only transitional to functional, why won't the functional stage only appear to be functional and not transitional to dysfunctional? And if the stage to be arrived at is itself actually transitional to dysfunctional down the line (so to speak), can it be (altogether or unequivocally) functional? Balkin has taken the trouble to inform his considerable readership that he rejects Hegel's view that history comes to an end; Balkin says he agrees with Heraclitus that one can't step into the same river twice.[39] (If history came to an end, one could step into the same river twice, at the end of history.) He has also said: "The Constitution is like Heraclitus's river."[40] If the Constitution could transition from dysfunctional to functional—simply, unequivocally, nontransitionally *functional*—it would have no future as dysfunctional. Being functional through time, it would remain the same in this respect, and in this respect one could step into the same river twice. But if Balkin is serious about not stepping into the same river twice, then Balkin can never attribute either functionality or dysfunctionality to the Constitution. Nor can Balkin coherently refer to "the other side" of dysfunctionality—much less predict that we'll get to that point. Nor can he coherently say that the nation is presently "mov[ing] between two constitutional regimes." One might guess that Balkin's inability to say any of these things explains his evasion of Greve's question.

But, seriously now, I know it's unfair to hold Balkin strictly accountable for what he says. I know he can't be serious about his "historicism." If he were serious about it, he wouldn't have much to say about anything, except, at the very most, that he couldn't say much about anything. The reason he couldn't say much about anything is that the language he would use to say something presupposes transhistorical things of several kinds. Take *snow*, for example; a serious historicist couldn't talk about snow. As a kind of thing, snow is distinguishable from its historical instantiations. Snow enjoys a stable existence that its historical instantiations lack. Individual snowflakes—things that happen in time—come and go; they crystalize now and then melt away, while snow as a kind of thing doesn't melt away. Even after the earth turns to Mars and there is no more snow anywhere, just as there are no more Passenger Pigeons anywhere, snow as a kind will still not melt into other kinds. Snow is signified by a word, "snow," that enjoys stability through time and that people use to pick out snow from other kinds of things in the world. As a kind of thing perceived by human beings (members of another kind of thing) with statistically normal perceptual equipment, snow has *qualities* (like *whiteness and coldness*) that also persist through time. Though these qualities would not exist absent beings with the requisite perceptual equipment, they are coeval with such beings, and therefore transhistorical relative to them. Snow has stable, and therefore transhistorical, *relationships* with other kinds of things; snow is *like* them or *unlike* them, in one or another respect. Snow, rain, and fog are all forms of precipitation, for example, for us today as for Homer, since the snow he described the better part of three millennia ago—along with the human types, relationships, and problems he portrayed—are (or undeniably seem) the same for him as for us. And finally, snow, injustice, revenge, lust, and everything else in and out of the world that we can have any inkling of have a quality whose nature is as hard to explain as it is impossible to deny: it can be talked about; it can be the subject of sentences. These sentences have meaning that some philosophers of language call *sentence meaning*. A locution's sentence meaning can be different from its meaning on particular historical occasions. "Snow is white" as a sentence means *snow is white*, whereas "snow is white" as an utterance on some particular occasion—that is, as a description of an event (an act of saying something) in historical time—can signify something else, like "blow up the bridge," or "I'm okay; let me in." Yet the sentence meaning of "snow is white" survives and must survive in the background of its utterance, whatever the intended meaning of its utterance. A speaker couldn't say blow up the bridge when I say snow is white unless both speaker and audience understood the sentence meaning of snow is white. Take historicism seriously across the board—that is, deny transhistorical meaning—and you're reduced to either silence or meaningless noise, which, in a communicative context, is equivalent to silence.

Balkin confirms this point, not by admission, to be sure, but by example. On those occasions when he waxes the serious historicist, he manages to say very little about what he wants to talk about. Balkin won't let himself say much about abortion rights, for example. He relates John Rawls's assertion in the 1990s that no reasonable person could deny a constitutional right to abortion in the first trimester. Balkin announces that he supports abortion rights. But, he says, "[w]e cannot know" what people in the future will believe. "We can only make arguments to each other in the present and have faith that we are on the right side of history and that, in the long run, our political values not only will gain general acceptance but also should gain general acceptance."[41] These statements are no more about abortion rights than Balkin's answer to Greve's question was an answer to Greve's question. They are instead statements about beliefs and hopes—statements about (1) what Balkin supports or "our political values," and (2) values that "will gain general acceptance" and that we believe should do so. Yet in our present context of disagreement about whether there really is a right to abortion, a statement about "abortion rights" would have to be (or presuppose) a normative statement—a statement that there really is or isn't a right to abortion. Rawls made such a statement—he talked about abortion rights, not his beliefs or hopes—when he said reason supports abortion in the first trimester and, implicitly, anyone who denies this is wrong and will be wrong.

Rawls of course could have been wrong and may yet prove to have been wrong, wrong all along; but he nevertheless said something about abortion rights. Balkin's statement falls short of this objective, for what values someone holds and what future values might gain general acceptance don't count and can't count as normative statements or as premises that can support normative conclusions. To have normative import, statements (1) and (2) require missing premises that no one accepts. In this case our premises would be: (3) everyone ought to believe what Rawls and Balkin believe; and (4) everyone today ought to believe whatever people generally will believe in the future. To say anything for or against abortion rights Balkin would need reasons based on generally shareable evidence, as opposed to privileged revelations, that a fetus at some or all stages of development *actually is or is not* a rights-bearing person, whatever anyone or even all of mankind might believe, has believed, will believe, or even can possibly believe about the matter. No one would undertake or seriously even attend to such an argument who did not assume a right answer to the question of the fetus's personhood. Historicists can't contribute much of any relevance to the debate, basically because historicism is a species of the (incoherent) doctrine that truth depends on what people believe. Yet as a matter of simple logic—today, yesterday, and tomorrow—there's no connection in reason between what people believe and what they ought to believe. In the end Balkin says much about what he and others believe and may yet believe. He also says, by way of implication, something that does have metaethical significance, namely, that moral truth is a matter of convention. But he says virtually nothing about the subject: whether abortion really is a right.

To the extent that Balkin does have something to say about constitutional issues he abandons historicism. The same holds for Levinson and value-skepticism. Both Balkin and Levinson have of course contributed a great deal to constitutional thought and especially to the subject of constitutional decay. Levinson is the present generation's leading voice for constitutional reform in the United States. But Levinson and Balkin have made their contributions not as value-skeptics or historicists. They've made their contributions in moments of forgetfulness, moments when they've forgotten unsupportable academic sophistries and lapsed into common sense. Noteworthy in the present context is their instrumentalist view of the Constitution.

As we've seen, Levinson has recently argued that the Constitution must be assessed in terms of the progress of constitutional government toward the public purposes listed in the preamble.[42] The government's deepening inadequacy to these ends has prompted Levinson's call for a constitutional convention made up of ordinary Americans chosen by lot explicitly for the purpose of avoiding the convention's domination by the well-off and, presumably, the super-educated. A most remarkable feature of this call is Levinson's open appeal to his readers' sense of obligation to their loved ones, their fellow citizens, and indeed their fellow human beings the world over. This may not be a call to revolution, Levinson says, but it is "at least a call to active citizenship," and by this he means citizens who can "ask the probing questions the Framers were willing to ask about the adequacy of their own institutions"—all for the sake of redeeming the promise of "'good government from reflection and choice.'"[43] Levinson thus sounds not unlike Murphy when he identified the capacity to change the Constitution as the preeminent constitutional virtue. Central to this capacity, said Murphy, is the existence in the community of people who can initiate action in the regime's behalf "in ways that cannot be precisely specified in advance" and "pass on to their children fidelity to the constitutional order's fundamental values."[44]

Balkin is even clearer than Levinson about the ends-orientation of his constitutionalism *and* its ultimate reliance on the character of the American people. Balkin argues in a recent book that the nation's fidelity to the Constitution depends ultimately on the redemption of the Constitution's promise of justice for all, including economic justice for all.[45] Since the actual pursuit of justice for all would depend on the attitudes and material resources of the American people, Balkin rests his hopes for constitutional success on the public-spiritedness of the American electorate.[46] In momentary lapses from his erstwhile historicism Balkin says that (1) *Dred Scott v. Sanford* (1857) and *Plessy v. Ferguson* (1898) were mistakes of constitutional reasoning—wrongly decided *in their day*— because (2) Americans *today* can't admit that these cases "reflect our nature or who we are."[47] This complex statement raises several questions. Is "today" something of a privileged moment from which we can categorically judge the past, an Hegelian "end of history," perhaps? In addition, who says *Plessy* doesn't "reflect our nature or who we are"? Has the Roberts Court not recently provided constitutional protection to racially motived "private" choices in derogation of the Warren Court's promise of equal educational opportunity?[48] Is declaring constitutional protection for race-based private choices regarding schools much different from what the General Assembly of Louisiana did in July, 1890, when it codified the race-based preferences of its white constituents regarding railroad cars? Moreover, is "who we are" to be decided by the most thoughtful and informed among us, thinkers not like John Roberts but like Jack Balkin? Does it matter in reason that John Roberts got to where he is through a process that involved the American electorate and Jack Balkin didn't? However we answer these questions, we should remember that only one of the eight participating justices dissented in *Plessy*, and for at least two generations beyond that decision the nation as a whole either supported or accepted white supremacist regimes concentrated in the southern states but hardly limited to them. When Balkin says *Plessy* was wrongly decided in its time because of what we (i.e., some of us) hold today about the morality of Jim Crow, he's applying a transhistorical standard, not one that confounds opinion with truth.

Not Altogether Hopeless?

I've imposed a pessimistic message on the reader even as I've admitted that offering this book for publication would be pointless if I had no hope whatever for American constitutionalism. I've touched on two broad justifications for pessimism in this chapter, one centering on political factors, like the way ideological division mixes with checks and balances to create what Francis Fukuyama aptly calls "vetocracy." I've also touched on intellectual barriers to successful thought about constitutional reform, like religious and

free-market zealotry and academic value-neutrality. Yet neither
area, the political nor the academic, is altogether lacking in hope-
ful signs. Though the American civil rights movement stalled a
generation ago and the Arab Spring died aborning, the astonishing success of the gay rights movement in the Western democracies over the past two decades lends some support to the faith of
Levinson, Balkin, and Seidman that constitutional reform could
conceivably come about through popular initiatives. And of the
several important writers in today's legal academy who recognize
the attitudinal sources of impending constitutional failure, some
are sufficiently independent of right-wing money and unburdened
by sectarian commitments, dated metaethics, and incoherent conceptions of liberalism to propose the active cultivation of liberal
virtues and thus to renew a strain of constitutionalist concern that
was well-recognized, if unprovided for, by Washington, Madison,
and Jefferson. Leaders among these writers over the last two decades include Michael Sandel, Stephen Macedo, and Stephen Elkin.[49] Walter Murphy argued forcefully in his final book that constitutional democracy could not survive unless "large numbers of
its people . . . internalize[d] enough of the regime's norms to act
willingly and, on occasion, even selflessly to promote" its "most
important . . . values," even at the expense of their "cultural differences."[50] Students and friends of Murphy have offered their own
versions of this message; they include James Fleming, Linda Mc-
Clain, and John Finn. Fleming and McClain argue for a version
of liberal constitutionalism in which government assumes an active role in promoting the civic virtues of self-responsibility, public
spiritedness, and respect for reasonable diversity in matters of personal morality.[51] Finn argues for expanding constitutional thought
beyond the rights orientation of litigators and jurists to include

the political scientist's concern for social results. His "civic constitutionalism" emphasizes a politically engaged and constitutionally conscious citizenry as essential to avoiding "constitutional rot."[52]

Among writers outside the Princeton circle that Murphy cultivated, Francis Fukuyama will soon publish a diagnosis of the nation's constitutional ills that places responsibility on "too much democracy" and the American tradition of hostility to government and bureaucratic elites.[53] Alan Wolfe's description of the cynicism and disengagement of the American electorate lends social-scientific support to Fukuyama's diagnosis.[54] Mann and Ornstein's account of Republican extremism serves as social-scientific support for Sandel's account of how radical ideologies move in to fill the spiritual vacuum left by the combination of value-neutrality and the headlong pursuit of wealth.[55]

Finally, George Thomas's forthcoming book on "the constitution of mind" will link current thought on constitutional dysfunction to Madison's call for a national university and the concern for cultivating a civic consciousness that stretches from the Founding to the present.[56] Madison's goal might be pursued today through a consortium of constitutional studies organizations, like Philadelphia's Jack Miller Center, and constitutional studies programs at several American colleges and universities, including Princeton, Yale, Boston College, and the University of Texas at Austin. These programs address regime questions not chiefly from the litigational perspective of lawyers and judges, but from what is essentially an ethically informed policy perspective: the concern for public purposes that typifies institutional designers and reformers. One can hope that these programs can avoid, or in some cases free themselves from, capture by right-wing forces. (I needn't mention the American left because it poses no threat to constitutional aspirations.) Constitutional scholars who would contribute to the survival of American constitutionalism must quit the business of celebrating the unworkable. They must come to see themselves as the American Framers saw themselves: less as constitutionists than as constitutionalists.

Notes

CHAPTER 1: WHY TALK ABOUT CONSTITUTIONAL FAILURE?

1. "Confidence in Institutions," Gallup, 6/4/2013, http://www.gallup
.com/poll/1597/Confidence-Institutions.aspx#1.

2. http://constitutioncenter.org/media/files/data_GfK_AP-NCC_Poll
_August_GfK_2012_Topline_FINAL_1st_release.pdf.

3. See Richard A. Epstein, *How Progressives Rewrote the Constitution*
(Washington, DC: Cato, 2006); Randy E. Barnett, *Restoring the Lost Constitution: The Presumption of Liberty* (Princeton, NJ: Princeton University
Press, 2004); Charles C. Johnson, "Silent Cal Speaks," *Claremont Review
of Books* 13, no. 1 (Winter 2012–2013).

4. Sanford Levinson, *Our Undemocratic Constitution: Where the Constitution Goes Wrong (And How We the People Can Correct It)* (New York:
Oxford University Press, 2006), 22–23.

5. See Alexander Hamilton, James Madison, and John Jay, *The Federalist*, ed. Jacob E. Cooke (Middletown, CT: Wesleyan University Press,
1961), 48:333–338; 49:341–343; 51:47–349. In this book, all subsequent refer-
ences to *The Federalist* will be in parentheses in the text, with the paper
number followed by a colon and the page numbers of Cooke's edition.

6. Jack M. Balkin, *Constitutional Redemption: Political Faith in an Unjust World* (Cambridge, MA: Harvard University Press, 2011), 2, 38, 42–43.

7. *Ex Parte Milligan*, 4 Wall. 2 (1866).

8. Robert A. Rutland, ed., *The Papers of James Madison* (Chicago: University of Chicago Press, 1977), 10:163–164, 209–214.

9. Sotirios A. Barber, *On What the Constitution Means* (Baltimore, MD: Johns Hopkins University Press, 1984) 49–50.

10. See Harvey Mansfield, "The Formal Constitution: A Comment on Sotirios A. Barber," *American Journal of Jurisprudence* 42 (1997):187–189.

11. See Sotirios A. Barber, *Welfare and the Constitution* (Princeton, NJ: Princeton University Press, 2003), esp. chap. 5.

CHAPTER 2: FAILURE AT WHAT KIND OF THING?

1. For an overview of *The Federalist* that highlights its instrumentalism, see Sotirios A. Barber and James E. Fleming, *Constitutional Interpretation: The Basic Questions* (New York: Oxford University Press, 2007), chap. 3.

2. See Pauline Maier, *Ratification: The People Debate the Constitution, 1787–1788* (New York: Simon & Schuster, 2010), 11–17; Calvin H. Johnson, *Righteous Anger at the Wicked States: The Meaning of the Founders' Constitution* (New York: Cambridge University Press, 2005), 1–4, 15–18.

3. See Sotirios A. Barber, *Welfare and the Constitution* (Princeton, NJ: Princeton University Press, 2003), 23–36.

4. 489 U.S. 189.

5. See David Currie, "Positive and Negative Constitutional Rights," *University of Chicago Law Review* 53 (1986): 864–872.

6. For an account of the far-flung and remarkably successful "Income Defense Industry" in the United States, and its methods for sheltering the wealthy from taxation, see Jeffrey A. Winters, *Oligarchy* (New York: Cambridge University Press, 2011), esp. 18–19, 213–224, 243–245, 272–273.

7. See Laurence H. Tribe, "The Puzzling Persistence of Processed-Based Constitutional Theories," *Yale Law Journal* 89 (1980): 1063; James E. Fleming, "A Critique of John Hart Ely's Quest for the Ultimate Constitutional Interpretation of Representative Democracy," *Michigan Law Review* 80 (1982): 634.

8. See Sotirios A. Barber, *The Fallacies of States Rights* (Cambridge, MA: Harvard University Press, 2013), 159–162.

9. See Ronald Dworkin, *Taking Rights Seriously* (Cambridge, MA: Harvard University Press, 1977), 134–135.

10. Robert Michael, *Holy Hatred: Christianity, Antisemitism, and the Holocaust* (Gordonsville, VA: Palgrave Macmillan, 2006), 129.

11. 494 U.S. 872.

12. See Randy E. Barnett, *Restoring the Lost Constitution: The Presumption of Liberty* (Princeton, NJ: Princeton University Press, 2004), 57–58, 60, 70, 79, 221–222.

13. 198 U.S. 45. The following argument borrows from Sotirios A. Barber, "Fallacies of Negative Constitutionalism," *Fordham Law Review* 75 (2006): 657–662.

14. See Barnett, *Lost Constitution*, 80–81.

CHAPTER 3: FAILURE AT WHAT, SPECIFICALLY?

1. Agreement on this last matter can no longer be taken for granted. It began to unravel when five justices of the Supreme Court decided the presidential election of 2000. It unraveled further with the "birther" campaign against President Barack Obama. Since a person's right to hold office depends in part on the legitimacy of her electorate, more unraveling could follow the spate of voter suppression laws by Republican-dominated state governments and the decision of five justices of the Supreme Court to cripple the Voting Rights Act of 1965; see *Shelby County v. Holder* (2013).

2. See Sotirios A. Barber and James E. Fleming, *Constitutional Interpretation: The Basic Questions* (New York: Oxford University Press, 2007), chap. 8.

3. Arguments against a pure proceduralism include: (1) the unintelligibility of means without ends; (2) the conceptual connection between choice and choice-worthy or good things, and the association of good things with ends, not means; (3) the etymological and semantic connections between procedure, method, and road and the impossibility of conceiving a road to nowhere or everywhere or a method of everything or nothing; and (4) the impossibility of choice among procedures save by reference to some substantive good like happiness, pleasure, or truth. To avoid these difficulties, process constitutionalists must connect their position to ends of some sort. To distinguish itself from positive constitutionalism, which conceives constitutional ends as public purposes, process constitutionalism substitutes private purposes. Yet the satisfaction of private purposes is not itself a private purpose; if it is a value it is a public value

and its philosophy is preference utilitarianism, a version of the common good. See Sotirios A. Barber, *Fallacies of States Rights* (Cambridge, MA: Harvard University Press, 2013) 18–19, 147–149, 197–198. The contest between positive constitutionalism and process constitutionalism is in reality a contest between two forms of utilitarianism: Benthamite or preference utilitarianism and Socratic or objective utilitarianism. Both assume that, as Aristotle says, all men act for what they think is some good. The preference utilitarian equates the good with the pleasant and assumes that what feels pleasant is pleasant. Socratic utilitarianism denies both that pleasure is the good and that each person is always fully aware of his or her wants. Socratic utilitarianism turns on a distinction between real and apparent goods and holds that no one really wants merely apparent goods. Socratic utilitarianism concludes that the only human life that makes perfect sense is the life of seeking knowledge of the good. If, on the other hand, pleasure is the good, and if humans act for what they think good, then the only reason for (performing the act of) accepting a philosophic doctrine would be the pleasure it brings. Yet the greatest happiness for the greatest number may demand much pain from those left out of that number, and whether any given person belongs in that number on any given occasion will depend on chance. On its own terms, therefore, preference utilitarianism is indefensible—that is, it is indefensible as a position that rational creatures should, in reason, accept. Even if preference utilitarianism were a true account about how people ought to behave, it could not recommend itself to rational actors generally, for its conception of the good precludes truth as a basis for action, and accepting or rejecting something is an action.

4. Martin Diamond, "The Federalist," in *History of Political Philosophy*, ed. Leo Strauss and Joseph Cropsey (Chicago: University of Chicago Press, 1972), 649–650.

5. Martin Diamond, "Ethics and Politics: The American Way," in *The Moral Foundations of the American Republic*, ed. Robert Horwitz (Charlottesville: University Press of Virginia, 1986), 99–104.

6. For Diamond's description of "the fully human life," see Martin Diamond, *As Far as Republican Principles Will Admit*, ed. William A. Schambra (Washington, DC: AEI Press, 1992), 327–328.

7. Ibid., 3–6, 12–14, 333–336.

8. Ibid., 281.

9. Robert E. Lane, *The Loss of Happiness in Market Democracies* (New

Haven, CT: Yale University Press, 2000), 6–8, 19–31, 67–71, 77–82, 102–109, 113–117, 319–337. Lane's findings are supplemented by research that indicates greater levels of subjective happiness in democracies that provide higher levels of state welfare services and support like medical care, old-age pensions, and protections for labor unions. See Benjamin Radcliff, *The Political Economy of Human Happiness: How Voters' Choices Determine the Quality of Life* (New York: Cambridge University Press, 2013), 51, 69, 123, 148–158.

10. *Lochner v. New York*, 198 U.S. 45 (1905).

11. Sotirios A. Barber, *Welfare and the Constitution* (Princeton, NJ: Princeton University Press, 2003), 61–62, 112, 135, 143, 145.

CHAPTER 4: CONSTITUTIONAL FAILURE: MOSTLY (THOUGH NOT ENTIRELY) ATTITUDINAL

1. Sanford Levinson is one of the few observers who believes that major constitutional reform is still possible. See his *Framed: America's Fifty-One Constitutions and the Crisis of Governance* (New York: Oxford University Press, 2012). I comment on this work in "Sanford Levinson and the Constitution's Future," *Tulsa Law Review* 49 (Winter 2013): 367–376.

2. See *Federalist* 62, at 416–417; Robert A. Rutland, ed., *Papers of James Madison* (Chicago: University of Chicago Press, 1977), 10:163–164 and 209–215.

3. Daniel Farber, *Lincoln's Constitution* (Chicago: University of Chicago Press, 2003), 17–18, 116–118, 132.

4. Ibid., 132–133, 138–140.

5. Ibid., 136–138, 142.

6. Ibid.

7. Ibid., 163–164, 169–170, 173–174, 188–192.

8. For Taney's opinion and the facts preceding it, see *Ex parte Merryman*, 17 Fed. Cases 144 (1861).

9. Abraham Lincoln, "Message to Congress in Special Session, July 4, 1861," reprinted in Steven B. Smith, ed., *The Writings of Abraham Lincoln* (New Haven, CT: Yale University Press, 2012), 340.

10. *Ex parte Merryman*, 17 Fed. Cases 144 (1861).

11. Lincoln, "Message of July 4, 1861," in Smith, *Lincoln's Writings*, 340.

12. See "Letter to Erastus Corning and Others" of June 12, 1863, re-

printed in Smith, *Lincoln's Writings*, 401, 402; and "Letter to Matthew Birchard and Others" of June 29, 1863, ibid., 408.

13. Farber, *Lincoln's Constitution*, 195.

14. Ibid., 196.

15. Ibid., 200.

16. Lincoln, "Message to Congress, July 4, 1861," in Smith, *Lincoln's Writings*, 345.

17. Ibid., 345–346.

18. William H. Herndon, *Herndon's Life of Lincoln* (New York: DaCapo, 1983), 304.

19. Abraham Lincoln, "On the Perpetuation of Our Political Institutions: Address to the Young Men's Lyceum of Springfield, Illinois, January 27, 1838," in Smith, *Lincoln's Writings*, 12. My comment on this speech is indebted to Harry V. Jaffa, *Crisis of the House Divided: An Interpretation of the Issues in the Lincoln-Douglas Debate* (Chicago: University of Chicago Press, 1959), 208–225.

20. On Lincoln's statement that he would abandon political ambition upon the restoration of the Missouri Compromise and its understanding of slavery as a necessary evil, to be confined to its existing borders, see Jaffa, *Crisis of the House Divided*, 219.

21. Jaffa proposes that obligation is "predicated upon . . . equality," and that, therefore, truly superior persons can't be obligated to their inferiors. The question in Lincoln's case is whether he seriously believed that some men were or could be superior to a point beyond the mutual obligations of civic life. Jaffa finds in Lincoln's speeches "a strong presumption in favor of an affirmative answer to this question." See ibid., 213–214.

22. For the possible "southern roots" of what is described as Lincoln's stubborn sense of honor, see Orville Vernon Burton, *The Age of Lincoln* (New York: Hill and Wang, 2007), 107–110.

23. Lincoln, "First Inaugural Address," in Smith, *Lincoln's Writings*, 324, 326, 327, 331, 332; "July 4th Message," in ibid., 335, 339, 346, 347.

24. James Madison, "Address to Congress, December 5, 1815," reprinted in Marvin Meyers, ed., *The Mind of the Founder: Sources of the Political Thought of James Madison* (Indianapolis, IN: Bobbs-Merrill, 1973), 388.

25. George Thomas explores the history and the theoretical implications of Madison's proposal in *Constituting the American Mind: The Found-*

ers and the Idea of a National University (Cambridge: Cambridge University Press, 2014).

26. Ibid., chap. 1.

27. See Herbert Storing, *What the Anti-Federalists Were For* (Chicago: University of Chicago Press, 1981), 21.

28. Gordon S. Wood, *The Creation of the American Republic: 1776–1787* (New York: Norton, 1972), 492, 501–502, 505, 509–510, 512–513.

29. Ibid., 517.

30. Thomas, *Constituting the American Mind*, chap. 1.

31. Stephen Macedo, *Diversity and Distrust: Civic Education in a Multicultural Democracy* (Cambridge, MA: Harvard University Press, 2000), 132.

32. Ibid., 40–43, 53–54.

33. Ibid., 63–72.

34. Ibid., 113, 125–127, 157–159.

35. Bob Pepperman Taylor, *Horace Mann's Troubling Legacy: The Education of Democratic Citizens* (Lawrence, KS: University Press of Kansas, 2010).

36. The judgment that power in the Senate, the Electoral College, and the amending process is unfairly apportioned assumes that the population of the United States constitutes one political community, not fifty or two or three. This is a reasonable assumption. As red as, say, Montana may be, one can surely assume that the average citizen of that state would not exchange her right (or her children's right) to move to, say, blue Oregon or purple Iowa, for Montana's right to exclude "outsiders" whose politics, religion, race, or sexual orientation differed from her own.

37. "Spreading Suppression: Restrictive Voting Laws across the United States," *Fair Elections Legal Network,* http://fairelectionsnetwork.com /spreading-suppression-restrictive-voting-laws-across-united-states.

38. Sohrab Ahmari, "Interview with Harvey Mansfield," *Wall Street Journal,* December 1, 2012, A13.

CHAPTER 5: CONSTITUTIONAL REFORM AND
CONSTITUTIONAL THOUGHT

1. Walter F. Murphy, *Constitutional Democracy: Creating and Maintaining a Just Political Order* (Baltimore, MD: Johns Hopkins University Press, 2007), 15–16.

2. Louis Michael Seidman, *On Constitutional Disobedience* (New York: Oxford University Press, 2012), 17, 19, 26-27, 46, 93-95, 115-116.

3. Ibid., 10, 12, 17-21, 143.

4. Louis Michael Seidman, "Let's Give Up on the Constitution," *New York Times*, December 31, 2012, A19.

5. Seidman, *Constitutional Disobedience*, 139-140.

6. Ibid., 140-141.

7. Ibid.

8. Robert Williamson and Elliot Zuckerman, eds., *Jacob Klein: Lectures and Essays* (Annapolis, MD: St. John's College Press, 1985), 114, 119-120, 125-126.

9. Sotirios A. Barber, "Promises, Axioms, and Constitutional Theory," *Tulsa Law Review* 48 (2012): 223, 228-233.

10. See Steven Macedo, *Diversity and Distrust* (Cambridge, MA: Harvard University Press, 2000), 69-72, 84-87, 151, 179-187.

11. *NFIB v. Sebelius*, 132 S.Ct. 2566 (2012). Chief Justice John Roberts successfully masked this radical overruling of *McCulloch v. Maryland* (1819) and *Gibbons v. Ogden* (1825) by upholding the ACA's "individual mandate" under Congress's taxing power. I argue against the states' rights conception of "limited government" in *The Fallacies of States' Rights* (Cambridge, MA: Harvard University Press, 2013), esp. chaps. 1, 4.

12. *Home Building and Loan Assn. v. Blaisdell*, 290 U.S. 398 (1934), upholding a state's mortgage moratorium law as an emergency measure in the teeth of the proscription in Article I, Section 10, of laws "impairing the Obligation of Contracts." *Bush v. Gore*, 531 U.S. 98 (2000). For an argument that *Bush v. Gore* violated the Constitution in order to save it, see Sotirios A. Barber and James E. Fleming, "War and the Constitution," in Mark Tushnet, *The Constitution in Wartime* (Durham, NC: Duke University Press, 2004).

13. Sotirios A. Barber, *On What the Constitution Means* (Baltimore, MD: Johns Hopkins University Press, 1984), 59-62, 114, 151.

14. For recent examples, see Jeremy Rabkin, "We Should Preserve, Protect, and Defend the Constitution—Not Trash It," in *Is the American Constitution Obsolete?*, ed. Thomas J. Main (Durham, NC: Carolina Academic Press, 2013), esp. 37-39; Charles R. Kessler, *I Am the Change: Barack Obama and the Crisis of Liberalism* (New York: Harper-Collins, 2012), 45-49, 69-88.

15. Francis Fukuyama, *Political Order and Political Decay* (New York:

Farrar, Straus and Giroux, forthcoming September 2014). For an advanced summary, see Francis Fukuyama, "The Ties That Used to Bind: The Decay of American Political Institutions," *American Interest*, December 8, 2013.

16. Seidman must mean something other than discursive disagreement when he says (at *Constitutional Disobedience*, 140): "Americans disagree about some matters all the way to the bottom, and the failure to recognize this fact entails a lack of respect for our adversaries." Discursive disagreement is always disagreement about a mutually presupposed truth-of-the-matter. For good-faith participants in discursive disagreement, this presupposed truth-of-the-matter is normative. Good-faith interlocutors implicitly agree about what counts as evidence and sound argumentation, and they implicitly agree to conform their opinions to wherever the evidence and the argument lead. Discursive disagreement in good faith exists in a framework of agreement that controls the disagreement that it enables. Discursive disagreement in good faith therefore cannot run "all the way to the bottom." It is no surprise, therefore, that Seidman eventually compromises his comment about disagreement "all the way to the bottom." At *Constitutional Disobedience*, 142, he calls on Americans to see their constitutional disagreements as disagreements about "aspirations that, at the broadest level of generality, everyone can embrace." I'd put the point in terms of distinctions between truth and opinion and real and apparent goods, with good-faith interlocutors seeking real goods, not just the apparent goods of the unexamined opinions they harbor going into good-faith debate. (Do good-faith interlocutors not disagree about what each assumes to be one and the same thing? Would their activity have a point if they assumed themselves infallible? Does anyone really want what one assumes is merely an apparent good?) In any case, and whatever your metaethics, the healthy politics that Seidman urges would be inconceivable if the country's present political division really did run "all the way to the bottom."

Of course, disagreement is not always "discursive disagreement in good faith." But where one encounters not good-faith argument that respects evidence and logic but bad-faith rhetoric contemptuous of evidence and logic, one can surely doubt an obligation of "respect for our adversaries." Whence the obligation to respect parties who won't listen to reason or who can't give reasons for their impositions on others? True, prudence can sometimes compromise honor and counsel a feigned respect for the likes of birthers, climate deniers, racists, homophobes, social Darwinists, and other forces of unreason. These elements may constitute the most numerous and powerful parts of one's community, and "respect" can connote "fear" as well as "admiration." But prudence is a switch hitter; at opportune moments it can swing sharply away from feigned respect all the way to open contempt, and beyond. It all depends on chances for success. In any case, Seidman is far from showing that reason has any genuine obligation to unreason.

17. Thomas E. Mann and Norman J. Ornstein, *It's Even Worse Than It Looks: How the American Constitutional System Collided with the New Politics of Extremism* (New York: Basic Books, 2012), xiv, 44–58; Alan Wolfe, *Does American Democracy Still Work?* (New Haven, CT: Yale University Press, 2006), 8–9, 19, 69–70, 82, 141–153, 173–179.

18. Nancy L. Rosenblum, "Governing beyond Imagination: The 'World Historical' Sources of Democratic Dysfunction," *Boston University Law Review* 94 (2014): 649; Michael S. Greve, "Fallacies of *Fallacies*," *Boston University Law Review* 94 (forthcoming 2014).

19. *Pierce v. Society of Sisters*, 268 U.S. 510 (1925).

20. *Meyer v. Nebraska*, 262 U.S. 390 (1923).

21. For an analysis of Levinson's ambivalence about the fact-value dichotomy, see Sotirios A. Barber, "Sanford Levinson and the Prospects for Constitutional Reform," *Tulsa Law Review* 49 (2013): 102, 106–111.

22. Jack Balkin, "The Last Days of Disco," transcript at 3, on file with the author.

23. Ibid., 26–27.

24. Ibid., 15.

25. Ibid., 3.

26. Ibid., 18.

27. 262 U.S. 390, 401 (1923).

28. Sanford Levinson, *Framed: America's Fifty-One Constitutions and the Crisis of Governance* (New York: Oxford University Press, 2012), 93.

29. Ibid.

30. Ibid., 58, 234–235, 326.

31. David Mayhew, *Parties and Policies: How the American Government Works* (New Haven, CT: Yale University Press, 2008), chaps. 4–5; R. Shep Melnick, "Does the Constitution Encourage Gridlock," in Main, *Is the American Constitution Obsolete?* 139–142.

32. Jeffrey Toobin, "Our Broken Constitution," *New Yorker*, December 9, 2014, 65.

33. Sanford V. Levinson, *Framed: Our Undemocratic Constitution: Where the Constitution Goes Wrong (And How We the People Can Correct It)* (New York: Oxford University Press, 2006). The quoted assessment is Lawrence Lessig's, dust jacket, *Framed*.

34. Levinson, "Thinking about Gridlock," in Main, *Is the American Constitution Obsolete?* 123–124 (emphasis in the original).

35. Levinson, *Framed*, 391–392.

36. See ibid., 8, 15, 55–57, 73, 115–116, 144, 146, 153, 280, 285, 316, 355–357, 393.

37. Ibid., 126–131.

38. Balkin, "The Last Days of Disco."

39. Jack M. Balkin, *Constitutional Redemption: Political Faith in an Unjust World* (Cambridge, MA: Harvard University Press, 2011), 1, 29.

40. Ibid., 62.

41. Ibid., 68.

42. Levinson, *Framed*, 8, 55, 115–116, 280, 285, 316, 355–358.

43. Ibid., 12–13, 32, 391.

44. Murphy, *Constitutional Democracy*, 342.

45. Balkin, *Constitutional Redemption*, 124–126.

46. Ibid., 8, 22, 33–35, 76, 80, 93, 250.

47. Ibid., 209–211; see also 17, 84, 243–246.

48. See *Parents Involved in Community Schools v. Seattle School District*, 552 U.S. 701, 720–721, 746–748 (2007).

49. Michael J. Sandel, *Democracy's Discontent: America in Search of a Public Philosophy* (Cambridge, MA: Harvard University Press, 1996), 128–133, 290–297, 324–328; Macedo, *Diversity and Distrust*, 10–12, 30–36, 125–130, 134–135, 181–187; Stephen L. Elkin, *Reconstructing the Commercial Republic* (Chicago: University of Chicago Press, 2006), esp. 60–73, 279–301.

50. Murphy, *Constitutional Democracy*, 342–343, and chap. 10 generally.

51. James E. Fleming and Linda C. McClain, *Ordered Liberty: Rights, Responsibilities, and Virtues* (Cambridge, MA: Harvard University Press, 2013), 4–11, 54–68, 87–93, 113–121.

52. John E. Finn, *Peopling the Constitution* (Lawrence, KS: University Press of Kansas, 2013), 29–31, 76–85, 93–95, 105–109, 215–218.

53. Fukuyama, "The Ties That Used to Bind," 1; compare Herbert J.

Storing, "Political Parties and the Bureaucracy," in *Political Parties U.S.A.*, ed. Robert A. Goldwin (Chicago: Rand McNally, 1964), esp. 151–156.

54. Wolfe, *Does American Democracy Still Work?*, chaps. 1, 2, 7.

55. Sandell, *Democracy's Discontent*, 24.

56. George Thomas, *Constituting the American Mind: The Founders and the Idea of a National University* (New York: Cambridge University Press, 2014), chaps. 1, 6.

Index